BUSINESS KEYS

KEYS TO INVESTING IN INTERNATIONAL STOCKS

Janet Lowe

BARRON'S

All inquiries should be addressed to:
Barron's Educational Series, Inc.
250 Wireless Boulevard
Hauppauge, New York 11788

Library of Congress Catalog Card No. 91-48228

International Standard Book No. 0-8120-4759-1

Library of Congress Cataloging-in-Publication Data

Lowe, Janet
    Keys to investing in international stocks / Janet Lowe.
        p.   cm. — (Barron's business keys)
    Includes index.
    ISBN 0-8120-4759-1
    1. Stock-exchange.   2. Stocks   3. Investments.
I. Title.   II. Series.
HG4551.L65 1992
332.63′22—dc20   91-48228
                                                                      CIP

PRINTED IN THE UNITED STATES OF AMERICA
2345 5500 987654321

CONTENTS

INTRODUCTION

Many United States investors gaze with curiosity and envy at the rise of capitalism in formerly Communist countries and the economic vitality in other parts of the world. Often they are inspired by what has gone on abroad in the past few decades. The examples are impressive.

- Since the 1960s, the Japanese stock market has risen above five times as fast as the U.S. market. Japan's has been the fastest growing economy in recent years, and it looks as if that country will continue to gain importance in various industries.
- Under former Prime Minister Margaret Thatcher, some of Great Britain's best companies were privatized and early investors have prospered.
- After generations of languishing in *protectionism,* guarding domestic producers at the expense of foreign companies, Mexico tore down the fences. During 1990, its stock exchange was one of the best performing anywhere.
- Although it still is tiny by most market standards, Chile's Bolsa de Comercio de Santiago soared 287 percent from 1985 to 1990.

What will happen as social and political reforms sweep Eastern Europe, South Africa, China, and many South American nations? The possibilities for investors abound.

Not only is the potential for profit expanding, but an ever larger share of the world stock market capitalization is found on foreign exchanges. In 1970, total stock market capitalization was $929 billion, and of that the United States held 66 percent. By 1990, total market capitalization grew to $8.4 trillion, but the United States accounted for about 32 percent of the market. Not surprisingly, cross-border equities trading almost doubled between 1987 and 1990. By the year 2000, nearly $5 trillion worth of cross-border trading is expected to take place.

Most investors will want to participate in foreign markets to achieve needed income and growth of investment assets. Even reluctant investors are almost forced into global markets, not only to hedge against swings in U.S. markets, but because so much important business is conducted abroad. Foreign companies hold key positions in many markets: the Japanese in automobiles and electronics, the Germans in manufacturing, the Canadians in lumber and paper, and the South Africans in gold mining.

The 1987 stock market crash and other recent events may lead investors to believe that world markets suffer from a "ripple effect," or move in tandem. This is not always the case. Growth and development are taking place at different speeds in different parts of the world; industrial sectors are impacted by world events in different ways; and the spirit of competition rears its head in unexpected places and ways.

Investors may be surprised to find they are already participating in foreign markets, perhaps through ownership of a multinational stock or through a U.S. stock mutual fund or a pension fund. Even conservative mutual fund portfolios contain the shares of foreign corporations.

Many investors are intrigued by the promise of global investing, but they don't have the knowledge to select, buy, sell, figure costs, settle taxes, or assess risk on foreign investments. This, of course, is no small job. There are 21 major world stock markets: Australia, Austria, Belgium, Canada, Denmark, Finland, France, Germany, Great Britain, Hong Kong, Italy, Japan, The Netherlands, New Zealand, Norway, Singapore/Malaysia, South Africa, Spain, Sweden, Switzerland, and the United States, and at least two dozen smaller and emerging markets.

Keys to Investing in International Stocks was written to help sort through the maze of information and opportunity.

Readers will notice that throughout the book, public corporations and mutual funds are mentioned by name and telephone numbers are frequently supplied for the open-end mutual funds. Specific investment vehicles, such as stocks, closed-end funds, and mutual funds, are included to illustrate a point and for the investor's convenience only. Every attempt has been made to ensure that these companies and funds are both reputable and well-established.

However, it is important to note that the inclusion of their names and numbers is not a recommendation to buy these shares or funds. Economic, financial, and investment conditions change continually. Any decision to buy, sell, or hold an investment must be made with the investor's individual goals in mind and in light of the most current information. (It is also important to seek the advice of an investment professional, particularly when you are considering international investments.)

1

MANAGING AN INTERNATIONAL STOCK PORTFOLIO

There are three paths to profit or loss from foreign stock market investments. As with domestic investments, the return on a stock is measured by

1. A rise or decline in the share price
2. Payments in regular or special dividends
3. Additionally, the value of a foreign investment will be affected by an escalating or falling foreign currency versus the U.S. dollar

There are four ways in which to invest abroad, each with advantages and disadvantages:

1. U.S. equity issues that have a strong multinational presence
2. Foreign stocks that are listed on U.S. exchanges and through American Depository Receipts (ADRs)
3. Direct purchase of foreign shares, either through a U.S. stockbroker or by opening a brokerage account in a foreign country
4. Mutual funds specializing in foreign stocks

When building a portfolio of individual stocks, the investor should

- determine if the company is on sound financial footing
- figure out if the shares are priced properly in relation to earnings and growth potential
- evaluate the special risks that accompany foreign investing, such as currency and economic and political risk.

The country of investment is often as important as the stock that is actually purchased. Each of the points just mentioned is covered in more detail in subsequent keys.

Investors who prefer to buy and hold stocks directly will find many excellent choices, although cautious investors may want to buy only a few, carefully selected international stocks. The limitation is the need to maintain adequate diversification. The number of different companies a portfolio should hold depends on the portfolio's monetary value. A small portfolio (up to $50,000) needs no more than 4 to 10 holdings; a larger portfolio should have 14 to 20 holdings.

The portfolio's value should be divided more or less evenly among the different companies. No more than one-fifth of the shares should be in foreign-based companies, although the component of foreign investment in a portfolio can be higher if the investment is by way of U.S.-based corporations with extensive foreign operations.

Mutual Funds. For those without the time or inclination to study and track foreign markets, mutual funds provide an alternative. Mutual funds also offer the advantages of diversification and professional management.

Mutual funds may be either closed- or open-ended. Many funds that focus on a country or region are closed-ended. *Closed-end funds* have a fixed number of shares, and once these are sold to investors, the shares trade on a major stock exchange. Usually closed-end funds trade at a discount to their asset value, ranging from 10 to 15 percent or more. As a general rule, investors should avoid paying a premium over net asset value (NAV) to get into a closed-end fund.

Open-end funds, those with an unlimited number of shares, are listed in many financial pages and can be bought either through a broker or directly from the investment company. Often the best bet for an investor is a no-load mutual fund with a solid track record.

There are a variety of funds, ranging from international and global funds to those that specialize in particular countries or regions of the world.

To select a mutual fund, consult the rankings that appear annually in major business magazines and quarterly in large daily newspapers. Compare performance, with special attention to the long term. Then, procure a copy of the mutual fund's *prospectus*. This document lists the fund's objectives and other essential information about the fund.

Most investment advisers suggest that at least 10 percent—but no more than 20 percent—of the value of a stock portfolio should be directed to foreign markets. If part of the portfolio is in high-quality U.S. multinational stocks, the percentage can be higher. As an investor becomes more experienced and skilled in dealing with foreign investments, the international weighting of a stock portfolio can be adjusted to match changing market conditions.

Revolutions, volcanic eruptions, hurricanes, and droughts can occur without warning and foil an otherwise brilliant investment plan. Diversification reduces the risk of international investing, regardless of whether the investment is in individual shares or some type of mutual fund. Choose investments so that the dollars are spread out by region, by country, by type of industry, and by company within an industry.

Because both the risk level and transaction costs of foreign investments are likely to be higher than those for domestic investments, foreign shares should always offer a specific advantage over a similar investment in the United States. (For tips on evaluating shares, see Key 19, Value Investing.)

2

CURRENCY RISK

Good management and great products often are not enough to ensure that a foreign company's shares move continually upward. When an investor buys the shares of companies abroad, fluctuations in *currency exchange rates*, the number of U.S. dollars that it takes to buy a foreign currency unit, can add to or detract from the total return. When the dollar strengthened against foreign currencies in the early 1980s, for example, U.S. investors in foreign securities suffered, even if the actual share price of the investments increased. In the late 1980s, the dollar's value declined and investors made fabulous gains.

In 1990, some stock markets lost value in terms of their own currencies but made impressive gains when investment returns were translated into U.S. dollars. For example, Great Britain's market slipped 0.6 percent but, in terms of the dollar, rose 22.2 percent. The French market declined 10.8 percent, but because of currency changes, U.S. investors showed a 9.4 percent gain.

The *currency impact* on foreign investments is confusing because the reverberations are the opposite of what they seem. When the value of the dollar drops against another currency, U.S. investors in foreign stocks cheer. The dollar's increasing power, on the other hand, can demolish the gains of U.S. investors in foreign markets. Only in markets in which the local currency is tied closely to the dollar or follows it—like Mexico, Hong Kong, and Singapore—are investors spared an adjustment when sales gains are converted back to dollars.

The confusion does not arise when the investment is made: a strong dollar then works in an investor's favor.

If the dollar has shifted in relation to the currency at the time of sale, however, the change must be considered.

For simplicity's sake, assume an investor buys one share in XYZ France at Fr10 (10 French francs) per share. At that time, the franc and the U.S. dollar are at a 1:1 ratio:

U.S.$1 = Fr1; therefore US$10 buys one share of XYZ France.

The dollar gets stronger. Now US$1 can buy Fr1.20. The price of XYZ has not changed, but the investor decides to sell anyway. He now finds that the Fr10 he gets from the sale will not buy as many dollars. He has lost US$1.70. If the dollar weakens by 20 cents (US$1 = Fr0.80), the investor discovers that his Fr10 is worth US$12.50 when reconverted.

Currency fluctuations can be tracked through the business pages of most daily newspapers. The *Financial Times*-Actuaries world indexes show the impact of currency changes on various stock markets both in terms of actual performance and in relation to the U.S. dollar. The FT charts are printed in many U.S. newspapers and investor magazines.

Currency exchange rates are quoted in two ways: (1) the foreign currency in dollars and the reverse, (2) the dollar in foreign currency. For example, on November 5, 1991, the British pound was quoted at £1.7710 to the dollar and US$0.5647 to the pound. Stated another way, it was possible on that day to buy US$1.7710 dollars for £1 (one pound sterling) or to buy £0.5647 for US$1.

Here is the trick. To figure the dollar value of the price of a share, you may use either figure. Simply remember to multiply when using the first number and divide when using the second.

Example. XYZ Corporation, now a British company, is selling for £15 per share on the International Stock Exchange in London. How much is it selling for in dollars?

£15 multiplied by 1.7710 = 26.565 (or, rounded off, US$26.56).

£15 divided by 0.5647 = 26.562 (or, rounded off, US$26.56: the slight difference is a result of the imperfection of the calculator.)

Even a minor shift in the rate can impact the price paid. For example, if the rate changed to US$1.7030 per pound and £0.5872 per dollar, the calculations would play out this way:

£15 multiplied by 1.7030 = 25.545, or US$25.54.

£15 divided by 0.5872 = 25.5449, or US$25.54.

In the second example, the U.S. dollar became stronger, or rose against the British pound. Consequently, the share price declined and the U.S. investor paid $1.02 less per share than was possible in the first example.

If the shares were purchased at the 1.7710 exchange rate and the rate moved to 1.7030 but the share price remained the same, the investor would show a loss on reconversion.

Rate movements of the U.S. dollar against a particular currency are difficult to forecast. Changes are determined in the international marketplace on the basis of supply and demand. If demand is high, the price rises. If it is low, the value of the dollar declines. Exchange rates are depressed by
• high inflation
• large trade and budget deficits

They are boosted by
• inflation control
• high interest rates unless interest rate hikes reflect economic chaos

Finally, political instability in any country can make its currency undesirable.

When dealing in American Depository Receipts or mutual funds, there is no need for currency calculations since they are already figured into the price. It is important to follow currency trends and anticipate changes when buying, selling, or holding *any* foreign investment.

3

INTEREST RATE RISK

Investors will remember that it was rising interest rates in West Germany and Japan that triggered the terrifying stock market crash of October 19, 1987. Before it was over, that calamity tumbled one foreign stock exchange after another. Investors reasoned that U.S. interest rates would also have to climb to keep foreign investors from pulling money out of the United States. They know that when interest rates rise, corporate profits suffer.

Furthermore, investors moved from stocks to safer and more lucrative interest-bearing securities, resulting in an exodus from the stock market and its eventual decline. The economic principles behind Black Monday apply internationally as well.

Throughout the world, countries attempt to use monetary policy to manipulate interest rates. Government and business leaders prefer low interest rates to allow borrowing for business expansion and to attract money into the stock markets for capital investment. Sometimes circumstances deem otherwise. A government must pay higher interest rates on government issues to attract the money it needs to finance public works projects, wars, or other affairs of state. Ironically, even booming economies present an interest rate risk, since flourishing commercial activity can breed inflation. In times of inflation, interest rate hikes are used as a tool to curb spending and cool off the economy.

Leaders of the world's largest nations, commonly called the *G-7 nations,* recently have had some success in stabilizing the international economy by discussing and coordinating monetary and interest rate policies.

Not only do interest rates impact share prices, they

also play a role in currency evaluation. One way of judging the riskiness of a currency is by the level of interest paid on a certificate of deposit (or its equivalent) in a bank in that country. The higher the interest paid in relation to CDs in other countries, the riskier the currency.

Investors should exercise caution when placing time deposits in countries where banks are paying high interest rates, because of the heightened currency risk.

Probably the easiest way to track foreign interest rates is by following the international columns of business publications, such as *The Wall Street Journal* or *Barron's*. *The Economist,* a weekly magazine published in London and available here, also carries key interest rates for countries around the world in its back pages.

4

INFLATION RISK

A high inflation rate is evidence of an economy under pressure or, when high enough, disarray. In 1991, as Russia dashed headlong toward capitalism, it was estimated that inflation in Moscow would reach an annual rate of 1000 percent! Economies with high inflation rates are unpredictable, and government intervention in banking and other key industries is not uncommon. Investment risk is intensified.

Inflation is a rise in the price of goods and services. Some level of inflation seems inevitable in growing economies, but anything more than three to five percent per year raises eyebrows.

Economics students are taught that inflation is caused either by too much spending or the profligate printing of currency. In other words, too much money is chasing too few goods and services. To fight inflation, *central banks,* through which governments administer monetary policy, often raise interest rates in the hope of making it more difficult to borrow money to buy things, thereby cooling off the economy. A decline in consumer and business spending tends to increase supply in the marketplace, driving prices lower, and thus curbing inflation. A rate increase in inflation rates also attracts money *away* from the stock market into bonds, certificates of deposit, or other interest-bearing instruments. Speculative investing, which often drives stock prices into an overpriced range, is restrained in the same way.

Because energy costs represent a large chunk of expenditures in healthy economies, investors often watch oil prices as an indicator of inflationary trends. Low oil prices help keep inflation rates moderate; high oil prices drive up the price of many goods and services higher.

9

Moderate inflation is often the result of rapid economic growth and is a prime concern of emerging economies and healthy, growing countries. On the other hand, *hyperinflation,* in which prices rise at 100 percent per year or more, can devastate financial assets like securities. People lose confidence in intangible assets or on-paper concepts, including securities and currency. Investors then shift their money to tangible, or *hard,* assets, such as real estate or gold, which traditionally maintain value in inflationary times.

A company's share price suffers in two ways during times of inflation. The cost of doing business is higher, thus leading to slimmer profits. Investors turn to companies that earn more money, which companies can either reinvest for future growth or share with investors in terms of dividends. Stocks have a more difficult time competing with interest-paying investments, such as corporate bonds and government securities. Countries with excessive interest rates invariably have troubled stock markets.

5

POLITICAL RISK

Peace and prosperity are more than a utopian wish: to an investor in anything other than defense industry stocks, they are essential. War destroys assets, disrupts industrial operations, and curtails imports, exports, and other activities vital to a healthy economy. For this reason, stock markets perform badly during times of political instability.

War, however, is not the only political risk. Even legitimate changes in leadership, an internal coup, or a revolution can mean a switch to an administration with different views of foreign investment.

When a conservative president is elected in the United States, for example, the stock market indexes often rise. When a liberal president takes office, the market contracts with a case of nerves. Under different administrations, tax regulations can change for better or worse, as can laws covering private property rights.

Germany, which has one of the most powerful economies in the world, was a favorite country for investors throughout the 1980s. Although most of the world cheered when the Berlin Wall was torn down and the two Germanies reunited, investors balked. The cost of reunification, they feared, would fall heavily on the German economy and would be reflected in corporate performance. Ultimately, Germany is likely to rebound with a larger work force, a larger consumer base, and greater productivity in the former East Germany.

Germany is also a first-rate example of how internationalization has changed the business climate. Many of Germany's most successful corporations sell their products around the globe and have worldwide manufacturing capacity. Events at home are important, but they are not the only factor in a company's success or failure.

An investor can get a fairly clear view of a country's political stability simply by reviewing its history and reading up on current events. On the basis of past experience, investors feel reasonably sure of political equilibrium in such countries as the United Kingdom, Canada, Japan, and The Netherlands. Investors can fairly accurately predict change, or at least uncertainty, in such places as India, Hong Kong, Iraq, and Cuba.

Remember the investor's maxim: The greater the risk, the greater potential reward.

Some of the most enriching investments have been in developing nations that have a rocky history but are solving their problems.

Several consulting firms, such as *The Economist, Intelligence Unit* and the *International Country Risk Guide,* specialize in rating country risk for professional investment managers. These calculations are sometimes reported in financial publications. Generally, risk ratings are formulated on an evaluation of interest rate and inflation risk, but also on

- credit and financial risk—based on a country's level of debt or the likelihood of default: a rising gross domestic product and a stable consumer price index generally signify a robust investment climate.
- political and policy risk—based on the consistency of government policy, the quality of economic management, the estimated level of corruption, and the mood of the public.
- disruptive external factors, such as weather patterns and the possibility of costly natural disasters

Failure in any of these areas can lead to government instability.

The goal of an investor is to understand the political risk, to determine if the level of risk is reflected in the price of the shares (higher risk, lower price), and to decide if the risk is tolerable.

The opposite of political risk is political opportunity, and in recent years government leaders in many countries have attempted to adopt free market economies, spur development, and welcome investment from many sources.

South America, Eastern Europe, and the Caribbean are regions that have long languished but are showing new vigor. Though direct stock investment is not yet feasible in Viet Nam, investors are watching with interest the normalization of trade with that country. If Viet Nam follows the lead of its neighbors, industrialization and stock market activity will follow. When political problems are confronted and solutions found, a country's economy and its stock market can improve dramatically.

6

NATIONALIZATION

At one time, the fear that governments would seize private assets was a major concern of corporate and private investors. In more than one instance companies have entered a country, drilled oil wells, built factories, or invested heavily in equipment—only to have everything confiscated by local authorities. When such a company is publicly owned, the shareholder ultimately loses.

In the last decade of the twentieth century, there has been a sudden awakening to the importance of private investment to national economies. A powerful shift is occurring away from managed economies, such as practiced by Communist countries. Many nations hope to move as much industrial activity as possible to the private sector.

Nationalization, the takeover of a private company's assets by a government, either with or without compensation, is considered an action of last resort. Nationalization is practical only when an operation must be preserved for the good of the public.

However, it is prudent to remember that the trend *away* from nationalization is new. As recently as 1981, the government of France fully nationalized 5 industrial groups, 36 banks, and 2 major financial holding companies. The goal of the French government was to preserve jobs that might have evaporated had free market forces prevailed.

Governments can easily resort to nationalization, especially when economies are under stress and entire industries need rescuing, regimes are threatened, egregious examples of mismanagement occur, fraud or price-gouging pops up in public service areas, or the populace believes that money and assets are being drained from a nation by a foreign power.

The greatest risk of nationalization exists in emerging countries, especially those that may have suffered from political or economic colonialism and that may harbor resentment toward outside influences.

Perhaps the greatest protection a corporation has against the nationalization of its assets is first, a careful political analysis of countries where investments are made and second, scrupulously fair and responsible management once an operation is underway. Investors should evaluate these same factors when choosing a company in which to invest.

7

HEDGING

Hedging is an investment technique used to offset investment risk by buying a second investment to offset a possible loss on a first. *Diversification* of investment purchases is one way to hedge potential losses in one market or a particular investment. Diversification follows the simple, age-old adage: Don't put all your eggs in one basket.

Diversification is a simple method of hedging. There are more sophisticated hedging systems, especially when currencies are involved. Very large investors often hedge against dollar fluctuations by:

- buying a reserve of foreign currency when they purchase foreign shares
- buying currency futures forward contracts
- investing in options

When buying reserves, investors protect themselves against currency risk by offsetting their equity position through an investment in the foreign exchange market. This type of hedging is based on the fact that when the U.S. dollar strengthens, foreign equity investments suffer but currency investments gain. If the dollar falls, an investment may fare well but the investor does less well on the currency transaction. (See Key 2, Currency Risk.) It is now possible to hold foreign currency accounts in some U.S. banks, making this sort of hedging easier.

With a currency future or forward contract, at the same time an investor purchases shares, she buys a forward contract in the foreign exchange market. The investor contracts to accept delivery on a certain number of marks, pounds, francs, or other currency at the current price, delivered at some future execution date. Currency forwards lock in a current rate for the future. As with direct currency investment, if the dollar strengthens against the foreign currency, the investor makes money on the forward, but may be hurt by the exchange rate when the stock is sold. The reverse, of course, is also true. Futures contracts are standardized, with set amounts and fixed delivery dates, and are traded on formal exchanges.

Currency options work in a similar way, except that the investor is only taking an option to buy on the foreign currency, rather than purchasing it. If the market goes against the investor, he or she can fail to exercise the option. The investor loses only the price paid for the option, which may be a lesser amount than if the actual currency had been purchased.

It is important to remember that hedging currencies can add to overall portfolio costs and has risks of its own. Some experts say there is no proof that it is worth the effort and expense over the long run. As a rule of thumb, unless an investor has more than 20 percent of a portfolio in a single foreign country, *currency hedging should not be considered at all.*

Hedge funds are mutual funds (not necessarily linked to global investments) that use hedging techniques, such as short selling, options, or trading in indexes, to make money in any market. They also are called *private investment partnerships*. Hedge funds trade with other mutual funds in the usual way, although the minimum investment is generally quite high. Again, some investment advisers say hedge funds are fraught with risk and of questionable effectiveness. (Consult professional investment advisers for more information.)

8

INTERNATIONAL PLAYS IN U.S. STOCKS

U.S. businesses have approximately $421 billion in direct investments outside national borders. The typical midsized U.S. corporation makes 25 percent of its sales abroad, and for the largest and most sophisticated multinational corporations, foreign sales run from 35 to 90 percent of the total. Often these companies report their fastest sales increases from abroad.

Why venture abroad on your own, when you can ride on the coattails of Coca-Cola, most of the Dow stocks, or other highly regarded U.S. corporations? After all, these companies have been importing, exporting, purchasing, and manufacturing abroad for many decades. They know the ropes.

- **Coca-Cola Company** operates in 160 countries and sells more than 45 percent of all the soft drinks in the world.
- **International Business Machines** is the largest foreign-owned company doing business in Japan.
- Despite increasing competition from abroad, **Boeing Corporation** remains the undisputed global leader in commercial aircraft manufacturing, and its planes fly virtually everywhere.

Spectacular gains in foreign markets may not be fully reflected in these shares, but buying U.S.-based multinational corporations is a relatively safe and satisfying way to participate in global markets.

Internationalization can make a dramatic difference to a company's bottom line and hence to its share price performance, as the Coca Cola Company demonstrates.

A $100 investment made in 1980 in Coca Cola stock, if dividends were reinvested, grew to $1211 by the end of the decade, outperforming the Standard and Poor's (S&P) 500 by more than 3:1. In 1989, a year when the U.S. stock market was off by nearly seven percent, Coke's share price gained 20 percent. Coke's steady surge forward can be attributed to its strategic global placement in the beverage industry.

The advantages of investing in U.S. stocks with a formidable foreign presence are many. The procedure is as simple and quick as placing an order with a local broker. Information is readily available on U.S. corporations in English, and accounting standards and financial disclosure rules are familiar to most investors. The yardsticks used for general investing, such as earnings growth, price/earnings ratio, dividend yield, price-to-book value, and cash flow estimates, are easily applied.

News regarding these companies is consistently reported in the press. Again, the managers of these companies are in an excellent position to study foreign markets and take advantage of changing economic situations. They are accustomed to dealing with foreign currency fluctuations and have systems in place to diminish currency risk and optimize profits.

The disadvantages of investing in U.S. multinationals are primarily linked to the *maximization of profits*. By targeting only those markets with the highest growth potential, investors can sometimes achieve the highest possible return. Because most of these corporations are still tied to the U.S. economy, events in the United States disproportionately impact earnings and profits. Because the companies are not specifically targeted to a high-growth area, such as Mexico or the Pacific Rim, the special benefits of the highest growth areas are diluted. Limiting exposure to U.S. companies would be to miss out on the investment opportunities presented by some astutely managed foreign companies that are positioned in key industries for the future. There is no exact U.S. equivalent, for example, for **Daimler-Benz, Unilever, Ajinomoto**, or **Mitsubishi Bank.**

How do you choose a U.S. corporation that makes an excellent international play? Look first to the best known brands in the world. Coca-Cola, **Kodak, Disney, McDonald's,** IBM, **Philip Morris's Marlboro** cigarettes and **Kraft Foods** are among the foremost. Each company's products are in demand in both developed and developing countries.

Next, look at the industries in which the United States is the world leader, such as aircraft, pharmaceuticals, and biotechnology. Boeing, **Merck & Company, E.I. du Pont de Nemours, Bristol-Myers Squibb** compete favorably worldwide.

Check annual reports and other literature on companies that seem like good investments. Measure their involvement overseas. **Johnson & Johnson, Tambrands**, and **Procter & Gamble** each enjoyed rapid growth in foreign sales in the past decade.

By following international business news, you will learn of promising developments in new business arenas and those companies that are making investments and signing contracts abroad. In recent years, for example, the press has carried stories about **Exxon** discovering deep-water oil fields far out in the Gulf of Mexico and negotiating a contract to explore for oil and gas off the coast of Siberia.

9

AMERICAN
DEPOSITORY
RECEIPTS

Once a curiosity to most U.S. investors, the *American Depository Receipt*—or ADR as it is commonly called—is an increasingly popular method of investing in specific international equities without engaging in complex arithmetic conversions. Investors simply buy and sell ADRs through the local broker, in the same way U.S. shares are purchased. ADR trading in 1990 surpassed previous records, with total volume valued at $125 billion. The majority of foreign shares sold in this country are ADRs.

The number of foreign companies seeking listing as ADRs is also growing. By the end of 1991, nearly 900 different ADRs were available to U.S. investors, compared to 585 in 1983.

ADRs are generally issued for widely held, actively traded issues. There are ADRs for corporations in countries ranging from Australia to Zambia, but the majority are businesses incorporated in Japan, Australia, or Western Europe. Foreign companies seek ADR listing for the prestige and convenience of trading on U.S. markets but also to tap into U.S. capital.

ADRs are listed on the New York Stock Exchange, and the American Stock Exchange, as well as on the National Association of Securities Dealers, Inc. automatic quote system (NASD), (NASDAQ). Unlisted ADRs are also sold over the counter through the *Pink Sheets*, a daily listing of market maker quotations, or through the OTC (over the counter) Bulletin Board Service. These unlisted pink sheet companies are usually small and unable to meet the listing requirements of the larger exchanges.

ADR stocks must meet special listing requirements, which are not the same as those for U.S. stocks listed directly on exchanges. Even though direct listing requires that companies meet more stringent standards, some foreign corporations, such as Mitsubishi Bank, arrange to directly list on U.S. exchanges. Mitsubishi Bank converted its accounting and reporting procedures to U.S. methods, which was both costly and time-consuming. However, the company's shares acquired greater prestige and were made more attractive to investors around the world.

The ADRs are priced in dollars and include the cost of administration and handling. An ADR is a negotiable receipt or certificate that often represents more than one share of stock, especially if the shares are low in price or if an exchange rate imbalance exists. By representing more shares, the ADR price is brought into line with typical share prices in the U.S. market.

The ADR certificate is issued by a depository bank or trust company, which holds the actual shares in a vault at its branch or a custodial bank (*custodial agent*) in the country of origin. There are two types of ADR dealers— sponsored and unsponsored. The *sponsored* facility works in cooperation with the issuing corporation and must pass along shareholder and voting information to the investor. The *unsponsored* ADR issuer buys and holds shares, sometimes without the agreement of the securities issuer, and has no obligation to pass along investor information.

An investor is entitled to all dividends and capital gains from ADR shares. In most countries, a withholding tax is levied on dividends paid to foreign investors. The tax is automatically deducted from ADR dividends by the custodial agent and the remainder passed on to the investor. (For more information, see Key 20, Tax Consequences.)

The primary ADR custodian banks are The Bank of New York, Banker's Trust Company, Chemical Bank,

Chase Manhattan Bank, Citibank, Morgan Guaranty Trust Company, and Bank of America. Each institution can provide a list of the ADRs they handle, and The Bank of New York compiles an annual booklet, *The Complete ADR Directory*. This may be available at a public library or at a brokerage firm library. For more information on the directory, contact The Bank of New York, ADR Division, 101 Barclay Street, 22W, New York, NY 10286. A roster of ADR stocks listed on the New York Stock Exchange can be found in Appendix A.

Some corporations also issue Continental Depository Receipts (CDRs) and European Depository Receipts (UDRs), which are traded in international markets similar to the way that ADRs are traded in the United States.

(For more details on ADRs, refer to Key 22, Reporting Requirements, and Key 24, Arbitrage.)

10

DIRECT PURCHASE OF FOREIGN SHARES

Investing in other countries through American Depository Receipts is convenient, but using ADRs alone may be somewhat limiting. Only about four percent of overseas stocks are available using ADRs.

U.S. investors can also consider buying shares in many foreign corporations directly through the major brokerage houses with foreign research facilities. Direct purchases can also be made through money-center banks, like Citibank, Manufacturers Hanover Trust Company, or Bank of America. The U.S. laws that separate banking and the securities industry do not apply in foreign countries, so many international banks trade for investors through branches abroad.

When an investor uses a brokerage house, he or she places an order with a broker, who then contacts a stock trader in the foreign country, who then makes the purchase. Under U.S. law, the value of the foreign shares must be listed on the customer's account in dollars and any dividend is also translated into dollars.

The stock certificate itself remains in the country, or it can be placed in the investor's name and forwarded, but this may take several months. Since the shares held in the investor's name cannot be sold until the investor signs and returns the certificate, opportunity to sell quickly may be lost. Many foreign shares are issued in *bearer form*, meaning that the investor's name does not appear on the certificate. The shares can then remain within the foreign country under a custodian and be sold without signature. If the stock certificates are lost or stolen, anyone who tenders them can sell them to a broker.

Finding information on foreign corporations is often a challenge. Some stocks that do not trade on U.S. markets—like Daimler-Benz of Germany are followed regularly in U.S. publications because of their international importance. Unfortunately, some very promising companies are relatively unknown in the United States.

Various international business directories, carried at most major libraries, list a U.S. office for foreign companies. Often, overseas corporations employ an investor relations officer or other official at their U.S. headquarters who can supply company reports printed in English. If this fails, a letter to corporate headquarters, even though it may be many thousands of miles away, usually elicits some form of corporate literature. Numerous foreign companies, especially those listed on the International Stock Exchange in London, routinely prepare financial reports in English.

Also, a wide selection of companies based abroad can be found in the *Value Line Investment Survey* or the Standard & Poor's stock report sheets. (See Keys 45, 46, and 47 for additional research sources.)

11

FOREIGN BROKERAGE ACCOUNTS

As world communications systems become more sophisticated and travel time shrinks, it becomes more and more workable to invest through a brokerage account in a foreign country. It is especially easy for U.S. citizens living near the Canadian and Mexican borders to participate in nearby marts. Airline crews, frequent business travelers, investors who are in military service, expatriates working abroad, and those who travel frequently for pleasure may want to explore foreign investment.

Whatever the circumstances, the U.S. customer must approach the foreign broker. Only brokerage firms listed with the Securities and Exchange Commission are permitted to solicit business from U.S. citizens. The investor must ask to buy a specific foreign stock. Even U.S. brokers are prohibited from advertising and recommending unregistered foreign shares to U.S. citizens. Although U.S. investors can buy foreign mutual funds, special Internal Revenue Service (IRS) tax provisions may make the practice unprofitable.

The advantage of making an overture to a foreign-based broker is dealing with a broker who is familiar with his or her domestic market practices and the local economy, industries, and specific corporations.

Since it is perfectly legal to hold foreign currencies and just as legal to own foreign bank accounts, payment is not a barrier. Another alternative for making settlements, which recently became possible in the United States, is to have a foreign currency-denominated account at a U.S. bank. However, only the more sophisticated banks set up such accounts.

The disadvantages of direct investing mostly have to do with the obstacles of dealing over long distances, coping with language differences, and unfamiliarity with foreign laws, investment practices, or tax requirements.

In certain countries, however, direct investment by individuals is impossible. Until 1992, Korea for example, prohibited foreign investment without government approval. In the past, many emerging growth countries were closed to outside investors and investment via closed-end funds was the only avenue, although the practice of excluding outside investors is fading.

In some countries, shares sell for prohibitively high prices. Swiss stocks, for example, frequently trade for as much as $2000 or more per share. However, exchanges with high share prices sometimes have smaller minimum purchase sizes than U.S. markets, where the norm is 100 shares to a round lot.

Generally, it is not advisable to have a direct foreign account for portfolios of less than $500,000 because of the costs of trading, currency exchange, and the higher risk level. In fact, foreign brokers sometimes refuse to handle smaller accounts. Of course, there are exceptions.

Whenever possible, it is wise to take possession of share certificates and to have payments made to a non-brokerage account. Foreign brokerage firms can go under, and all too often, accounts are not insured. Inquire about commissions, account insurance, taxes, and trading costs, since practices vary from country to country.

In addition to the $500,000 minimum account size, investors setting up foreign brokerage accounts must maintain detailed records. Since U.S. citizens have occasionally attempted to evade taxes by using these types of accounts, the Internal Revenue Service is alert to any infraction.

12

U.S. STOCKS LISTED ON FOREIGN EXCHANGES

More than 200 U.S. multinational corporations, plus many smaller and secondary stocks, trade on foreign exchanges. Among the 20 largest shares listed on the Toronto and Montreal exchanges are IBM, **General Motors Corporation, Ford Motor Company,** and McDonald's. Philip Morris, IBM, Exxon, and numerous others can be found on the Tokyo stock exchange. **Citicorp** is listed on the New York, Midwest, and Pacific stock exchanges in the United States and on the London, Amsterdam, Tokyo, Zurich, Geneva, Basel, Toronto, Dusseldorf, and Frankfort exchanges.

Furthermore, large trades by international investors in U.S. stocks are sometimes executed on London's International Stock Exchange after the New York Stock Exchange (NYSE) closes. New York closing prices are used, but the trading volume never shows up on the NYSE.

Many ADR stocks also reflect the influence of multiple exchange action. Besides trading on eight Japanese regional exchanges, **Matsushita Electric Industrial Company** is listed on the New York and Pacific exchanges, as well as the Amsterdam, Frankfurt, Dusseldorf, and Paris exchanges. Unilever trades on the NYSE, plus exchanges in the Netherlands, Great Britain, Austria, Belgium, France, Germany, Luxembourg, and Switzerland.

These companies list themselves abroad to attract foreign capital and to increase liquidity for their shares. Also, many companies have major operations in the countries where they are listed. They have employees, contractors, suppliers, bankers, and customers. There is as much interest in the company and its destiny in the foreign country as there is at home.

Corporations usually list the markets in which they trade in their annual reports, frequently near the back.

These multiple-listed companies are pioneers in the 24-hour trading concept, in that their shares are almost always being bought and sold somewhere in the world. (See Key 17, Twenty-four Hour Trading.)

This means several things to the international investor:

- Corporations can raise capital in markets virtually anywhere, increasing their ability to support growth by equity financing.
- Investors enjoy greater liquidity because ownership is spread among more shareholders.
- Share prices, even for U.S. stocks, are constantly influenced by other markets and economic conditions in other countries. A market dive in Tokyo can damage the share price of Philip Morris, IBM, or Citicorp. Hard times in London might force investors to sell U.S. shares and thus edge down the price, regardless of the outlook for the individual companies. On the other hand, enthusiasm for a company in foreign markets can propel the U.S. price skyward.
- Finally, whenever shares trade on more than one exchange, the opportunity for arbitrage trading arises. (For more information on arbitrage trading, see Key 24.)

13

GLOBAL VERSUS INTERNATIONAL STOCK FUNDS

Global equity funds invest in securities traded anywhere in the world, including the United States. *International funds,* on the other hand, can hold stocks from any country in the world with the *exception* of the United States. While global funds offer the greatest possible diversification, international funds serve as a better hedge against volatility in the U.S. markets than global funds, since their holdings mostly come from overseas exchanges.

On average, however, global funds reward investors more abundantly than international funds. In 1991, global funds offered an average total return of 19.5 percent, but international funds achieved a 12.3 percent average total return. For the five years ending in 1991, global funds racked up a 60.5 percent average total return but international funds achieved a 50.8 percent return. The message seems to be that the wider the choice of stocks from which an investment manager can choose, the stronger a fund's performance is likely to be. The same principle applies to individual stock investors, which is a good reason to aim for a global investment portfolio.

Some funds use the word *international* in their name but do not strictly limit themselves to securities outside the United States. To be categorized as an international fund, two-thirds of a portfolio must be invested in shares of non-U.S. companies. Read the fund's description, prospectus, and list of holdings to be certain of the manager's investment strategy.

Because they are more diversified in their holdings and because fund managers can switch quickly out of trouble spots, global and international funds are likely to be less volatile than country or regional funds. Overall, however, both global and international funds tend to be riskier than U.S. mutual fund investments because they add exchange rate risk to the general investment risk.

Some global and international funds specialize in certain industries, such as precious metals, biotechnology, or pharmaceuticals (See Key 23, Sector Investing.) Other global and international funds may specialize in certain types of markets, such as emerging (third world) markets. Of course, the less developed a market is, the chancier a fund will be. However, profits in emerging markets sometimes soar far above those of established economies.

There are about 110 international funds available and 38 global mutual funds. Fund performance is closely tracked in the financial press.

The following global funds have established track records:

Oppenheimer Global Fund (800) 525-7048
Putnam Global Growth Fund (800) 225-2465
Templeton World Fund (800) 237-0738

Some well-established international funds are:
Fidelity International Growth & Income Fund (800) 523-1919
G.T. International Growth Fund (800) 824-1580
Scudder International Fund (800) 225-2470 or (800) 225-5163

14

COUNTRY FUNDS

Nearly three dozen country funds are available in the United States, specializing in everything from staid European nations to high-flying emerging economies. These funds offer the classic advantages of mutual fund investment while allowing the investor to choose the economies he or she believes will boom in the years to come.

Country funds also offer an avenue to investment in such countries as Korea and Taiwan, where individual investors only recently have been able to buy stock. Additionally, shares in some countries trade for exceptionally high prices by U.S. standards. Many individual investors would not be able to afford them, except through a fund.

Country mutual funds are of two types—*closed-end funds* that trade like stocks, and *open-end funds* that are bought and sold in the same way as most mutual funds.

Many *country funds* are closed-end investment companies, a type of fund in which a fixed number of shares are sold to the public. After the initial sale, the investment company shares trade on a stock exchange rather than being listed with other mutual funds.

Despite the fact that investors must pay a broker's fee when buying a closed-end fund, performance can compensate for the additional cost. In 1991, closed-end stock funds brought investors a 41 percent return, compared to 30.7 percent for mutual funds.

Investment advisers warn against buying closed-end funds that trade at prices above their *net asset value* (NAV) per share. The NAV is the worth of a fund's assets, minus its liabilities, divided by the number of shares outstanding. A fund selling at a discount of more than 10 percent below net asset value is considered a good investment. The ideal time to buy is after a market slump, when the fund may be trading up to a 30 percent discount to net asset value.

A list of closed-end funds is published weekly in *Barron's,* in the Monday edition of *The Wall Street Journal,* and in the Saturday edition of *The New York Times.* The newspaper listings include the fund's net asset value, the stock price, and the percentage of difference between them. Technical data on closed-end funds are offered by *Value Line* and Standard & Poor's investment service.

Prices of open-ended funds appear in the mutual fund listings in most newspaper financial pages. Additional data, including a list of addresses and toll-free telephone numbers of mutual fund investment companies, can be requested from the Investment Company Institute, 1600 M Street, NW, Washington, DC 20036 (202) 293-7700.

Several precautions must be taken when investing in country funds. Because liquidity is poor in some foreign stocks, be prepared to buy and hold country funds for the long term. Be prepared for volatility. Country funds are notorious for spectacular gains and painful losses.

The bet here is on the country, not a specific industry or corporation. Study and, if possible, travel to the country in question. The investor can then get a sense of the nation's political stability and measure how far along a country is in its development. Investors should use criteria for country funds similar to those used in acquiring other funds. Check the track record, although many country funds are relatively new and long-term records may not exist. Diversify into several regions of the world.

Closed-end funds include the **Germany, Swiss Helvetia, First Iberian, Indonesia, Korea, Malaysia, ROC Taiwan, Singapore, Spain, Thai Capital,** and **Mexico Equity and Income** funds. Closed-end funds are listed on exchanges and can be purchased through a stockbroker.

Perhaps the best known and established open-ended country fund is the **Japan Fund**, (800) 225-2470 and (800) 225-5163. It began as a closed-end fund, but later converted. Others are: **EquiFund, United Kingdom National Fiduciary Equity Fund**, (800) 225-6265 and **Fidelity Canada Fund**, (800) 544-8888 and (800) 523-1919.

15

REGIONAL FUNDS

By placing their investment dollars in regional funds, investors can encourage positive change and help supply capital to newly thriving or about to thrive regions. Investors can make the best investment advantage of such developments as the creation of the European Economic Community (EC), regional trade agreements, such as the Association of Southeast Asian Nations (ASEAN), or political, social, and economic conditions, such as low wage rates in Southeast Asia, pent-up consumer appetite in China, or the development of oil in South America.

In terms of risk and opportunity for profit, regional funds fall somewhere between country funds and international funds. They allow greater company, industry, and exchange rate diversification than country funds because there are more stocks to choose from, but less flexibility in moving out of lagging markets than international funds, because choices are fewer.

Several closed-end regional funds trade like stocks. These are listed on exchanges and are purchased through brokers. (For a more detailed description of closed-end funds, see Key 14, Country Funds.)

Among the closed-end regional funds are the:

Asia Pacific Fund
Europe Fund
Latin America

Among the open-ended regional funds are

Alliance New Europe, (800) 221-5672
Merrill Lynch Pacific Fund, (800) 637-3863
Nomura Pacific Basin Fund, (800) 883-0018

16

OFFSHORE FUNDS

An *offshore mutual fund* has headquarters *outside* the United States. Often the funds are legally domiciled in the Bahamas, the Cayman Islands, or another country where few if any regulations exist regarding mutual fund operations. U.S.-based multinational corporations including mutual fund companies, sometimes have legitimate uses for offshore financial operations, but the concept should raise a red flag for cautious investors.

The rationale sometimes offered for organizing a fund offshore is to avoid burdensome rules or taxes like those in the United States, Great Britain, or other developed countries. It is prudent to remember that U.S. investors are required to report investment income to the Internal Revenue Service, regardless of the country where it was earned.

To be legally sold in the United States, offshore funds must be registered with the Securities and Exchange Commission (SEC) and heed all other applicable federal and state regulations. Offshore funds do not always do so.

Some fund operations eventually turn out to be Ponzi schemes or another form of investment fraud. Over the years, certain offshore fund organizers have discovered ways to market within U.S. borders, eventually fleecing investors of hundreds of millions of dollars. For awhile it was fashionable for fund organizers to describe themselves as "liquid real estate funds." The name alone should be a tip-off, since real estate is among the least liquid forms of investment.

The SEC is responsible for ensuring that mutual funds disclose all pertinent information in their prospectuses and do not engage in misleading, unfair, or illegal practices.

Investors, however, should take the time and effort to obtain a prospectus and check the track record and the management of any mutual fund being considered for purchase. Be particularly leery of any investment—foreign or otherwise—sold over the telephone, since "boiler room" operations and other high-pressure sales tactics often are used to market questionable investment vehicles.

Offshore financial havens include Bermuda, Montserrat, Antigua and certain other Caribbean Islands, the Cook Islands in the Pacific Ocean, and the Channel Islands off the coast of France.

17

TWENTY-FOUR HOUR TRADING

Perhaps no segment of business is as directly impacted by the relentless march of technology and the subsequent globalization of business as the securities industry. Twenty-four hour trading is a reality for portions of the industry and a strong likelihood for everyone else. Many international corporations are listed on multiple exchanges, such as the New York Stock Exchange, the Pacific Stock Exchange in California, the International Stock Exchange in London, the Hong Kong and Tokyo stock exchanges, and perhaps an exchange in Australia or New Zealand. More than 200 U.S. stocks, both large and small in capitalization, are listed on exchanges outside the United States. Even without the benefit of advanced technology, these shares are being bought and sold around the clock somewhere in the world. Technology is being installed that can actually link many marketplaces to one another, making 24-hour trading as easy as an ordinary domestic buy or sell transaction.

The New York Stock Exchange in June 1991 began a two-year experiment allowing limited after-hours trading that, in effect, extended market hours until 5:15 P.M. Eastern Standard Time (EST). The goal of the NYSE was to recapture business that had been lost to foreign exchanges.

The National Association of Securities Dealers, Inc. (NASD) has long been preparing its electronic trading system for just such an eventuality. The NASD automatic quote (NASDAQ) over-the-counter system was expanded to the United Kingdom in 1991, allowing securities firms, investors, and world-class companies to participate in a new transatlantic market for U.S. equities. The NASD in 1991 won SEC approval to begin trading some stocks at 3:30 A.M. in the United States to coincide with the opening of London's market. NASD has forged ties with smaller world exchanges as well.

The American Stock Exchange, Reuters, and the Chicago Board Options Exchange are discussing full-blown 24-hour trading systems with the SEC.

The move toward around-the-clock, global stock trading is also being facilitated by the worldwide trend toward uniform electronic settlement systems. At the same time, government regulators around the world are working to bring their securities regulations up to the demands of global traders. The International Organization of Securities Commissions (IOSC) meets periodically to discuss establishing more uniform worldwide standards of capital safety requirements for securities firms and other crucial issues.

Around-the-clock trading also transpires on what is called the *"fourth" market* of the United States, a network of institutional investment managers who buy and sell directly to one another via computer systems. The Instinet Corporation Crossing Network and the Portfolio System for Institutional Trading (POSIT) exist primarily to conduct the business of institutions as they continually adjust their portfolio positions. These trades take place entirely off the exchanges, after hours, although their prices may be based on the closing prices on the New York or other U.S. stock exchanges. At this time, however, the volumes traded on these systems are relatively small—Instinet traded 625 million shares in 1990—but the possibility for future volume is vast.

The after-hours business sessions are especially useful to investors who want to trade on significant corporate and other news that breaks at odd times. Investors everywhere can respond to a natural disaster that strikes at midnight, wars that erupt at 6 A.M. EST, or even atypical trading on a distant exchange.

Not everyone in the United States welcomes extended U.S. exchange hours. The New York Stock Exchange was badgered into abandoning its plans for earlier opening hours by West Coast securities industry professionals, who already start work at 6:30 A.M. to be at their desks for the NYSE opening bell. Extra burdens are placed on all investors when they must track their investments at various hours in distant markets.

However, nonstop stock trading may be inevitable, forced into place by investors in parts of the world once considered remote and out of the main stream of stock-market activity.

Once 24-hour trading is in place, the next advance in stock markets will be a uniform worldwide marketplace. The barriers to a truly integrated international mart are technical. Only natural resistance to change, regional cultures, laws, and old animosities prevent the implementation of such a progressive concept.

18

PRIVATIZATION

Some of the best investment opportunities abroad occur when governments decide to sell assets to private investors—commonly referred to as the process of *privatization* or *denationalization* of public property. Governments take this step for two reasons: (1) to increase efficiency and/or (2) to raise funds for government operations.

The trend toward privatization stems from the belief that private industry tends to manage business operations more capably and at a lower cost than governments, thus enhancing the economy in general.

Sometimes a government sells a telephone company or some other operating unit simply to raise money to pay off debt or finance other public programs. Not only does the government profit from the sale price, but once an industry, public utility, transportation system, or some other operation is privatized, it can also be taxed to raise more revenues.

Privatization started gaining in popularity in the late 1970s and 1980s. By the early 1990s, nations around the globe were rushing to sell everything from airlines to liquor distilleries to zoos. Some of the most successful privatized entities have been telephone companies and other public utilities. Usually, these companies operate as monopolies with the ability to set rates high enough to ensure a profit.

Often, privatized companies simply go public by selling shares to investors. Sometimes shares are sold only to residents of the home country, but occasionally they are available to outside investors as well. *Prior subscriptions* (advance purchase of shares) may be available, with the usual risks that accompany initial public offerings. Once the sale is complete, shares may be traded in the usual ways.

In other cases, governments sell factories or other operations directly to an existing corporation. One way to take advantage of the privatization trend is to buy shares in a company that may be acquiring newly privatized property. The management of an experienced company is in a good position to evaluate the quality of the asset, to estimate future profits from it, and to manage the resource once it is acquired.

Western automobile manufacturers, such as **Fiat** and **General Motors,** have purchased automobile plants in Eastern Europe; **Procter & Gamble** bought a soap maker in Czechoslovakia, and several U.S. telephone companies acquired ownership of privatized telephone companies in Latin America and the South Pacific.

One highly successful privatization effort combined several strategies. The **Telecom Corporation of New Zealand** was sold by its government to two regional U.S. telephone companies, **Ameritech** and **Bell Atlantic,** with the agreement that they would reduce their ownership to 49.9 percent within three years. The U.S. companies then took Telecom Corporation public in New Zealand and in international markets simultaneously, combining several markets in a single public offering. The day it went public, Telecom Corporation ADRs were the most actively traded stock on the New York Stock Exchange. The offering was structured in this way because the government of New Zealand knew it had the best chance of raising the money it needed from global investors.

In many cases, early investors have done well in privatized companies. As with any investment, however, there have been exceptions. There may be unforeseen problems with a company or a national economy. Once a privatized company is listed, it may lose its *"protected"* or government-preferred status and become subject to the slings and arrows of competition faced by all other public corporations.

In certain cases, governments retain a controlling interest in the privatized company, making it difficult for the company to throw off the ropes of bureaucracy and take full advantage of the efficiencies of private ownership.

For an example of that happening, see Key 28 on Japan's giant Nippon Telephone and Telegraph (NTT). (The opposite of privatization is the risk of nationalization. See Key 6.)

19

VALUE INVESTING

In the late 1980s, when the prices of shares listed on the Tokyo Stock Exchange reached stratospheric levels, it was popular to say that Japanese equities could not be measured by the same yardsticks used for U.S. stocks. Perhaps not, but astute investors know that every asset has its proper price, and Japanese stocks are no exception.

A smart buyer never pays more for something than its worth. Determining the right price to pay for U.S. corporate shares is no cinch. Estimating the value of foreign stocks is even more problematic. (See Key 21, Accounting Differences.)

Brokers often talk about *total return* (share price growth plus dividends), but this is a historical figure and may not apply to the future. Once an investor has decided a company is in a promising industry and has considered the special risks related to international investments, the appropriate price for the shares must be determined. There are three important measures of the present value of a stock:

1. *Dividend yield* is the dividend per share a company is paying, divided into the price of a share: from 1.5 to 10 percent is a normal range by U.S. standards, and higher is better.
2. *Price/earnings ratio* is the price of a share divided by the earnings per share. In the United States, the typical P/E may be from 10:1 to 30:1: lower is better. In Japan, P/Es in the range of 200:1 are not unusual. To bring Japanese ratios into line, many analysts simply add 20% to earnings to compensate for accounting and other differences. By doing so,

the P/E ratio is likely to fall more closely in line with U.S. stocks.

3. *Book value* is the worth of a company's tangible assets, minus liabilities, divided by the number of shares outstanding. A book value significantly higher than the share price is suspect; a price lower than the share price connotes a bargain.

Only the first measure, dividend yield is reliable on the face of it. The price/earnings ratio is partially believable. We know the price of a stock, but companies around the world shift earnings from quarter to quarter or year to year for tax and other reasons. Book value is also mysterious and open to manipulation, since even in the United States it is typical to list assets at their historical value. For long-established companies that bought properties years ago, assets may be understated. For companies with variable-rate loans, liabilities soar when interest rates escalate. Although each measure of value is imperfect, these criteria remain useful. In foreign shares, as with U.S. companies, dividend yield, P/E ratio, and book value give the investor yardsticks by which to evaluate a stock purchase.

Make use of all three:

- Compare them to the figures for similar companies throughout the world. If you can find a better deal elsewhere, it may be a good idea to take it.
- Compare to other companies within the same industry. Companies within the same industry groups tend to move in similar cycles. An industry in a low cycle could be poised for an upward movement in share price. The company in the industry with the most favorable fundamentals could move fastest and highest.
- Compare to other companies within the same country or region. P/E ratios in the Caribbean, for example, are exceptionally low by U.S. standards. In Japan, as noted earlier, they are extraordinarily high.
- Compare the company's current numbers to the past. Is the company improving, stagnant, or falling back? Why? If the figures are flat because of placid management, this is not good, but if earnings are repressed

because of major investments in new equipment, the company may be preparing for a rosier future.

Additionally, investors want to know that a company has the wherewithal to be what accountants call a "going concern." Is the company's cash flow sufficient to cover all its expenses, with a reserve for unexpected events? How does the company's debt compare to its equity? Ordinarily, debt levels should be half the equity level.

This information may be culled from company documents, from analysts' reports, or from various research services. Keys 45 and 46 give more details on research and information sources.

This homework may seem burdensome, but it is necessary and fascinating. The most successful investors in the world are value investors.

20

TAX CONSEQUENCES

When a government decides to encourage foreign investment, one of the first things it does is examine the tax laws and ensure that its revenue policies do not deter new investment. This process works. When Austria decreased dividend withholding in the mid-1980s, new money flowed into the market.

Tax obligations come in twos for the global investor—the taxes levied by the country where the investment is made, and domestic taxes.

Practices vary enormously in foreign countries but sometimes are mitigated by a tax treaty with the United States. Most nations impose no capital gains tax but levy a withholding tax on dividends paid to foreign investors. The tax averages about 15 percent in most countries. Your stockbroker should be able to explain the tax laws in the country in which you are investing, or at least be able to locate the information. Several of the guidebooks listed in Keys 46 and 47 include tax rules and tax treaties for specific countries.

In the case of ADRs and mutual fund investments the process is simplified. Foreign taxes are deducted before dividends and capital gains are paid to the investor.

Investing outside the United States is not a legal way to escape taxes. A U.S. citizen must declare all dividends, capital gains, or any other profit on an investment.

However, the investor is generally not taxed twice. To offset the taxes already paid, the investor may file Form 1116 for a foreign tax credit on U.S. federal returns.

The formula for computing a foreign tax credit is too complex to be described here, especially if investments are made in more than one country. The IRS estimates that it takes 41 minutes to read the instructions for Form 1116, and one hour and 26 minutes for the typical taxpayer to fill out the form. The IRS can supply instructions for computing the tax. The Internal Revenue Service expects the investor to maintain records and report results in U.S. dollars. If exchange rates are recorded at the time the securities are purchased, when dividends are paid, and again when the securities are sold, record keeping should pose no problem.

An announcement by a government that tax laws or treaties are being modified in favor of foreign investors is a most sincere indication that outside investment is being encouraged. Eventually, such a change could lead to a more robust stock market.

21

ACCOUNTING DIFFERENCES

Japanese corporations often do not take the earnings or debt obligations of certain subsidiaries into consideration on their financial statements, making it difficult to accurately evaluate the indebtedness or the earnings of a Japanese company. In Europe, higher taxes lead to thrifty accounting and earnings may be understated. In each instance, corporate finance officers can argue convincingly that they are using the best accepted procedures for their own countries. Correct as they may be, accounting standards around the world remain a hodgepodge. Developed countries are confusingly different from one another, and a large percentage of the emerging economies need to be brought up to global standards. These differences present a challenge for the international investor.

When balance sheet figures cannot be compared, it becomes difficult to understand the advantages or disadvantages of one company over another. What is the meaning of a price/earnings ratio if earnings are not calculated the same way from company to company? Is there any significance to debt/equity ratios if subsidiaries are included in one country when they are 49 percent or more owned but excluded in another country regardless of percentage of ownership? Probably not. Investment decisions, with their apples to oranges comparisons, take on an added dimension of guesswork.

As economic reforms and the move toward internationalization sweep the globe, emerging countries are attempting to bring their stock markets up to the highest international standards. Many countries have voluntarily adopted the Financial Accounting Standards Board

(FASB) practices common in the United States. Some smaller markets, including Brazil, Chile, Mexico, India, South Korea, Malaysia, and the Philippines, now follow sound procedures. Because they intend to become truly global players, certain foreign-based corporations have voluntarily adopted U.S. generally accepted accounting procedures (GAAP).

A London-based group, the International Accounting Standards Committee (IASC), upon encouragement from the International Organization of Securities Commissioners, is preparing an internationally accepted set of accounting rules. Although most countries have not yet agreed to adopt the simplified and more flexible procedures, many have agreed to give them serious consideration. Once countries begin adopting the guidelines, investors will benefit from uniformity in corporate financial accounting standards.

22

REPORTING REQUIREMENTS

When Robert Maxwell, chairman of the **Mirror Group**, died in the sea near his yacht in 1991, the cause of his death was cloaked in mystery. As it turned out, Maxwell's passing was not the only puzzle. In the weeks before his death the media baron allegedly moved assets from public companies to family enterprises, stripping worth from already debt-ridden shareholder-owned entities to protect private companies.

How could Maxwell have hoped to get away with it? Experts say that accounting rules and disclosure of information to shareholders in Great Britain are so lax that facts can be concealed there that U.S. shareholders would have a right to know. The United Kingdom is not the only country that has weak reporting rules, and even in countries with stronger regulations, regulators sometimes let down their guard and fraud occurs.

One of the problems of investing in foreign stocks is that the level and frequency of required financial disclosure to regulatory agencies vary enormously from country to country. Disclosure can also be different for various American Depository Receipt shares. In most cases, foreign disclosure standards are not as stringent as they are in the United States, and in some countries the regulations for foreign stocks trading on their home markets are not vigorously enforced.

Outside the United States, corporate financial reporting to regulators is required less often. In the United States, sales, earnings, and other data are reported quarterly. In most other markets, financial reporting is required only twice a year, and even then, late filings are common. Many corporate leaders say that the U.S. fixation—and preference for frequent reports on financial conditions only encourages a short-term perspective on investments. In Switzerland, financial disclosure is required on an annual basis and most Swiss companies are quite sound.

Many ADRs trade in the less regulated, over-the-counter market or on the Pink Sheets because the companies are not willing to comply with U.S. disclosure rules. These shares are not quoted in the newspaper, but prices are available from brokerage houses.

Although foreign issuers of listed ADRs are technically required to report financial information to the Securities and Exchange Commission, this requirement became effective only in 1983. Issuers who began trading on U.S. exchanges before that time have been *grandfathered,* granted an exemption, and in other cases, the requirement is waived altogether. The SEC estimates 43 percent of the foreign issuers of ADRs do not provide current information to the commission. Some of the most respected foreign corporations, including **Fuji-Photo Film, Inc., Toyota**, and **Nissan Motor Corporation,** are grandfathered and exempt from reporting.

In the case of most ADR stocks, the ADR certificate doubles as a prospectus, and other than what an investor is able to ferret out, he or she may receive few other details about the company.

Additionally, with ADR shares the sponsoring organization that handles the ADR transaction is not required to report (and seldom does) the currency conversion rate used or the fees and expenses deducted by the depository institution or others before payment.

The ADR investor, however, must report certain information to the SEC. Whether they are U.S. citizens or foreign nationals, investors must notify the SEC if more than five percent of a company's shares are acquired, including purchases of shares via ADRs.

The SEC has been studying the ADR system to determine if disclosure procedures are adequate, especially in light of heightened trading in this area. Once the study is complete, some rules may be eased and others could be made tighter.

Not only are the United Kingdom and other nations reviewing their disclosure rules to better protect investors, but as mentioned earlier, efforts are also underway to make financial disclosure more uniform worldwide. In the European Community a goal has been set to "harmonize" the stock markets. The International Organization of Securities Commissions has been created by various government agencies to establish global consistency. The Federation de Internationale des Bourses de Valeurs in Paris, representing the world's stock exchanges, also advocates the development of mutually compatible standards and practices.

The effort to make international trading more comparable and easier has made some rules less stringent rather than more so. Until the 1990s, corporations that wanted to raise money in the United States, still the strongest capital market in the world, had to conform to U.S. rules and regulations. Many foreign companies were doing so voluntarily. However, the Securities and Exchange Commission, to make it easier for foreign countries to sell stocks to institutional investors in the United States, waived disclosure rules. Robert Maxwell's Mirror Group, taking advantage of the waiver, sold $85 million in shares to U.S. investors the year before his death. After his empire unraveled, the shares turned out to be worth much less.

Insider trading, stock manipulation, and other subterfuge that pits outside investors against insiders is not necessarily prevented by strict rules on financial disclosure. As the stock exchanges of the world become more global in their operations, however, governments realize that for investors to have confidence in markets, unfair activity must be prevented. Japan, Australia, Switzerland, and dozens of smaller countries in recent years have adopted or are considering insider trading bans and have stepped up surveillance of domestic securities markets.

23

SECTOR INVESTING

One of the most important reasons for investing in international equities is to find the best companies in a particular industry. A *sector* refers to a particular group of stocks, usually in a single industry or closely related industries. For example, airlines, automobiles, oil, chemicals, and electronics manufacturing are sectors.

If an investor foresees a particular trend in development, he or she may want to direct investment money toward a related industry sector.

Say an investor realizes that the baby boom generation will rush to have children of their own, and she wants to make investments based on this knowledge.

She may buy the shares of a toy, diaper, or infant formula manufacturer. Or if she anticipates that airlines around the world will want to replace fleets of aging airplanes, she will buy stock in aircraft-manufacturing companies and their suppliers. Since it is difficult to anticipate which toys or airplanes will be most popular and which companies will plan best for the deluge of sales, the smart investor might want to spread his or her money among various toy or aircraft companies.

It would be nearly impossible to be a sector investor in oil shares without studying the venerable foreign giants, **British Petroleum** or **Royal Dutch Petroleum Company**. Toyota, Nissan, **Honda,** Daimler-Benz, and Fiat all play important roles in the automotive business. Banks, such as Mitsubishi Bank, **Sumitomo Bank**, and **Deutsche Bank** will be key to the capital markets of the future. Corporations from around the world are represented in the electronics, computer, chemical, and pharmaceutical industries.

Drug companies, for example, are viewed as sector stocks with a resistance to recession. The largest pharmaceutical companies, Bristol-Myers, Squibb and Merck & Company, have global sales, but they also have impressive international competition. **Glaxo Holdings** and **Smith Kline Beecham** are based in Great Britain. **Ciba-Geigy** is based in Switzerland, and **Rhone-Poulenc** is French. Each has been a favorite with investors.

Country funds and regional funds are another form of sector investing (see Keys 14 and 15), allowing investors to express their confidence in the economic vitality of one part of the world over another. As with any other approach to investment, diversification into several fields and into several countries or regions is prudent.

24

ARBITRAGE

In the economist's ideal world, identical items should sell for identical prices everywhere. Experienced investors, just as experienced grocery shoppers, know that identical pricing is seldom the case. Investors also perceive that any time there is a discrepancy between securities prices in different trading arenas, an *arbitrage opportunity* arises. That is, investors can buy lower priced shares in one market and sell them for a profit in the higher priced market.

At times, for instance, a sufficient *spread* (difference in price) develops between the price of a security in its domestic market and the ADR price in the United States. This spread, or *price differential*, can be caused by poor dissemination of news about a stock or different reactions to the news in different countries. Active traders sell ADRs, for example, if after transaction costs are considered the ADR is trading at a *premium* (higher price) to the deposited security that stands behind the ADR. This kind of a disparity is a signal that the ADR price will very shortly come down.

Conversely, if an ADR is selling at a *discount* (lower price) to the deposited security (again figuring in the transaction costs), the arbitrageur purchases ADRs in the United States. He or she then withdraws the deposited securities from the ADR facility and sells them at a profit in a foreign market.

This is obviously not an easy trick for the average investor. It could require traveling to the country where the stock is held in a vault and arranging the transaction, or doing so through an agent. Arbitrage requires quick action to take advantage of momentary market disparities. However, since large investors (such as institutions) more readily have the resources and networks to orchestrate fast trades, it does happen.

Arbitrage, in fact, acts as a balancing force in the market. Ultimately, arbitrage limits the degree to which ADR prices (or the share price of stocks listed directly) in U.S. markets diverge from prices in the home market or other foreign markets for the security.

Arbitrage is particularly common with gold shares (see Key 43), since they are quoted in New York and London and usually in Johannesburg. As more and more corporations are listed on exchanges around the world, arbitrage trading between different markets is likely to increase, especially among larger and more sophisticated investors.

25

SPECULATION

Investors who love a horse race or thrill to the roll of the dice can get a similar rush from global investing. However, there is a distinct difference between gambling and speculative investing. Gambling is based on random outcome. Speculation assumes a risk in anticipation of gain but recognizes a high possibility of loss. *Speculation* depends on the ability to analyze certain fundamental information related to an investment. Professional investors often realize long-term profits from speculation, but also hedge possible losses through short selling, options, future contracts, and other insurance mechanisms.

Certain types of ventures, such as oil, gas, and gold exploration, have throughout history been financed through speculative capital. Venture capital is also raised from investors willing to take exceptional risk. *Venture capital* is capital raised and used to underwrite new companies in many fields, most notably biotechnology, electronics, and other high-technology fields. Venture capital is often granted in the form of a loan, although sometimes it is attached to equity in the company. The venture capitalist who holds equity expects his or her investment to become liquid and reaps a reward when the company's share price scores a meteoric rise.

Specific foreign markets, such as the Vancouver Stock Exchange in Canada, specialize in raising venture capital and trading speculative types of shares. Other markets, like that of Jamaica, are speculative because of their extreme price swings. Between 1984 and 1987, Jamaica's stock index leapt 700 percent. After the 1987 market crash, the index lost a third of its value, sliding to its 1988 low. By 1990 Jamaican stocks rebounded to 15 percent above their 1987 high.

An important distinction exists between a disappointed speculative venture capitalist and the victim of an investment scam. Scams are sometimes touted as speculative ventures with the possibility of sensational profits. In a scam, however, there is little or no possibility of investor profit, since the organizers are draining the investments directly into their pockets. Because investment scams are often designed around speculative activities, such as oil, gas, or gold shares, commodities or currency arbitrage, it is important to take the time and effort to investigate any investment being offered and to thoroughly check the legitimacy of the organizers. Any sales pitch promising an exceptionally high rate of return should be carefully scrutinized.

Calls to the Better Business Bureau, the district attorney, a local FBI office, or the regional office of the SEC can be revealing. The NASD can also tell you if they are investigating a brokerage or other investment company. These regulatory organizations have divisions specializing in investment fraud.

However, if a fraudulent operation is new on the scene, even the authorities may not know about it. Common sense must prevail. As a rule of thumb, avoid buying investments offered over the telephone by unknown salespersons. In general, it is best to conduct business through an established, well-known brokerage house.

Speculation can serve as an important market function. Although speculation exists in all markets, the largest number of speculative ventures can be found on the smallest and most volatile exchanges in the developing countries. In 1990, the International Finance Corporation reported that 1200 companies raised more than $22 billion from new issues in emerging economies.

Individual investors may have difficulty buying and selling in obscure marts, but mutual funds employ experts to study specific stocks and swings in local markets. Those investors interested in mutual funds with a speculative proclivity and unusually high profits should study those designated growth or aggressive growth funds, emerging companies funds, or precious metals and gold funds.

26

JAPANESE STOCK EXCHANGES

With a gross national product of $2.8 trillion, Japan is the world's second largest economy behind the United States. In recent years, everyone has wanted to play Japan's *mane gemu*, or money game. The stock markets there trade the shares of more than 2500 companies, and in 1989, the total capitalization of the Tokyo Stock Exchange exceeded that of the New York Stock Exchange for the first time. During the 1980s, Japan's leading stock market indicator made an astonishing 5.7-fold advance, making Japan's one of the most impressive stories of the decade. Then, showing investors that its markets could be as vulnerable as any other, Japan entered a decline. Investors in the Japanese stock market were brought back to reality as the market fell about 4.5 percent in the last quarter of 1991. Foreign investors account for 9 percent of the trading in the lively Tokyo-led Japanese exchanges.

In all, there are eight exchanges in Japan, although Tokyo, which handles more than 80 percent of the total business, is the most important. The others are in Kyoto, Niigata, Osaka, Hiroshima, Sapporo, Nagoya, and Fukuoka. Each exchange is subject to the Securities and Exchange Law, which was patterned after U.S. laws and is administered by the Ministry of Finance.

There are three well-defined sections to the chief exchanges. The first tier is made up of the larger listed companies, which account for about 96 percent of the total market capitalization. The second section includes shares that are newly quoted or shares that otherwise would be traded over-the-counter. The third is strictly over-the-counter. Traded on the Japanese exchanges are ordinary, preferred, and deferred shares, shares to be retired with profits, shares without voting rights, convertible shares, convertible debentures, debentures with right of preemption in respect of new shares, and separable warrant debenture bonds.

There are four types of settlement when trading shares: (1) *regular settlement,* the most common, requires delivery on the third day of business following the contract; (2) *cash settlement* calls for same-day or next-day delivery; (3) *special agreement* allows delivery on an agreed-upon date but no more than 14 days following the contract; and (4) *when issued settlement* is used for new shares and subscription rights and is on a date fixed by the exchange.

Some trading practices are prohibited in Tokyo. It is not possible to sell short, for example, because it is illegal to sell shares not already owned.

Brokerage commissions are based on a sliding scale depending on the size of purchase but range from 0.15 percent for large transactions to 1.2 percent for small. The minimum commission is ¥2500, or approximately US$19.00. Shares on Japanese exchanges usually sell for such low prices that a round lot is often 1000 shares.

There is no limit to the amount of investment foreigners can make in Japanese corporations unless the industry is classified as in the national interest. If so, shareholding is limited to 25 percent. This extensive protected list includes mining, agriculture, nuclear power, gas, railway, banking, aircraft, pharmaceuticals, and oil refining. Furthermore, foreign investors are required to hire a Japanese agent to exercise their proxy rights.

Critics of Japanese stock markets say the market is more speculative than those in the United States and Europe, and the scandals of the early 1990s have given some credence to the belief that outsiders are discriminated against. Certainly some practices are different. Under Japan's *keiretsu* tradition of industry cartels, associated corporations hold shares in one another's companies. These shares are seldom traded, thus giving a certain stability to share prices and affording protection from unwanted takeovers.

Some of the best-known companies to trade in Japan are **Industrial Bank of Japan, Tokyo Electric Power, Nippon Telephone and Telegraph** (see Key 28), Toyota, Matsushita Electrical Industrial Company, **Hitachi,** Ltd., and **Toshiba**. Most of Japan's leading corporations trade in U.S. markets as ADR shares.

The **Japan OTC Fund** is a closed-end fund and concentrates on smaller and newer Japanese companies. The Japan Fund, established 29 years ago, is one of the oldest country funds around. It is an open-end fund.

Japan Fund, Inc., (800) 221-8120 or (800) 225-5163
G.T. Japan Growth Fund, (800) 824-1580

27

NIKKEI STOCK AVERAGE

In the 1980s, eyes popped in the United States when the so-called Nikkei Dow reached astronomical levels. In 1981, when the Dow-Jones Industrial Average was trading around 1000, the Nikkei Average was 7681.84. By January 1991, the DJIA had risen to about 2508 but the Nikkei was up to 22,487. The Japanese indicator is extremely high compared to the Dow-Jones Industrial Average, but the numbers are not necessarily comparable because of the way the index is constructed. The Nikkei, which is computed in yen, is also misleading because of currency translations. Furthermore, because it is a broad index, the Nikkei Average is more wisely compared to the S&P Stock Index than to the DJIA.

The Nikkei Stock Average (225), as it is properly called, is the best known, most frequently used market indicator for the Japanese stock markets. It is not the only one, though. The Nikkei 500 Stocks Average (formerly called the Nikkei–Dow-Jones 500) provides stock averages based on 500 representative companies. The Nikkei Over-the-Counter Average is for shares not listed on the Tokyo Stock Exchange. The OTC indicator was initiated in 1985 by the Nihon Keizai Shimbun Company.

The Tokyo Stock Exchange Average (Topix) is considered the most representative indicator of the total market. The Topix was based on a value of 100 for the average of all listed shares on the indicator's opening day in 1968. The average is adjusted regularly for new listings and changes in capital.

The Nikkei 225, however, remains the most prominent indicator. Established in 1949 as the Nikkei Dow-Jones Stock Average, the opening average was 176.21. The index was restructured in 1975 and renamed in 1985. The Nikkei Average is the arithmetic mean of the stock prices of 225 representative issues, multiplied by a constant that is often adjusted.

Some of the familiar corporations listed in the Nikkei Index are **Mitsui Mining, Shimizu Construction, Fujita, Asahi** and **Kirin** breweries, **Fuji-Photo Film, Inc.**, Hitachi, Ltd., **Mitsubishi Heavy Industries,** Toshiba, **Fujitsu, Ltd.**, and **Sony Corporation.**

The procedure for calculating the Nikkei Stock Average is as follows:

$$\text{Nikkei Stock Average} = \frac{\text{Aggregate of the 225 stock prices}}{\text{divisor}}$$

Originally, the divisor was 225. It has been lowered over the years. The divisor is adjusted when any of the stocks is replaced or has exercised its rights for stock splits or gratis issues. It is done this way:

$$D = d \times \frac{A - W}{A}$$

$$= A - \text{aggregate of theoretical stock prices ex-rights}$$

Such that: D = new divisor
d = divisor before adjustment
A = aggregate of stock prices with rights
W = value of rights

The stock price ex-rights is calculated in the following way:

Theoretical stock prices ex-rights = T
Capital contribution = C
Ratio of capital contribution to par value = R
Right for subscription per share = S

$$T = \frac{A + C \times R}{1 + S} \text{ (both subscription and free distribution)}$$

When companies are dropped or added:
Rights price = stock prices of dropped companies minus stock prices of added companies

28

THE WORLD'S LARGEST CAPITALIZED COMPANY

Like a beefy sumo wrestler, Japan's foremost telephone company, Nippon Telephone and Telegraph (**Nippon Denshin Denwa** in Japanese), weighs in as the world's largest public company, with a 1990 stock market capitalization of $96.7 billion. Stock market capitalization means that if the total number of common shares outstanding is multiplied by the share price, this is what the company would be worth if sold on the open market. Impressive: yet the public utility tends to prove the adage that the best things come in small packages. Until 1986, NTT was wholly owned by the Japanese Ministry of Finance. What followed became a legend in the securities industry.

When the ministry announced in 1985 that the company would be privatized, the shares were given a par value of ¥50,000, or about US$310. Investor response to the offering was astonishing, with bids made for nearly six times the number of shares available. As a result, the initial price per share was set at ¥1.197 million, or about US$7,480. The right to buy the shares was determined by public lottery, despite that the NTT price/earnings ratio was 130. At one point the P/E multiple reached 270 and the NTT market capitalization grew to 11 percent of the entire Tokyo Stock Exchange. Its value surpassed the total capitalization of the West German and the Hong Kong stock markets combined. The capitalization eventually abated to about 2 percent of the Tokyo market's total value, still enough to make an inordinate impact on the Nikkei Stock Average.

The company has since earned a reputation as a notoriously sluggish investment. When it comes to sales and profits, many companies were larger and livelier. By 1991 the price had dropped 53 percent from the initial offering price. Additionally, the dividend offered a yield on only 0.66 percent.

However, the Japanese government took steps to improve the NTT stock market performance. In the fall of 1991, the Ministry of Posts and Telecommunications announced that it would reverse its policy of limiting investments in NTT to Japanese nationals. Foreigners will be allowed to hold up to 20 percent of the outstanding shares of the company. NTT said at that time that it would also explore listing its shares on foreign exchanges.

The ministry's announcement came during a phase when Japan was being criticized for blocking outsiders from financial participation and when NTT shares were trading near an all-time low. Under pressure from new competition in a deregulating telecommunications marketplace, NTT was cutting rates and trimming staff and planned to spin off a computer subsidiary. NTT also began expanding into overseas markets and acquiring new technology.

Despite the lackluster stock performance, NTT is one of Japan's most respected and influential business entities. It has considerable research and development capability, and close government connections and is part of a powerful business family (*kieretsu*) that includes NEC Corporation, Fujitsu, Ltd., and Hitachi, Ltd.

In 1991 NTT had about 1.7 million private shareholders, but the Ministry of Finance held 66 percent of the 15.6 million shares. Additional public offerings of NTT shares still held by the Ministry of Finance were expected to follow.

29

THE EAFE INDEX

An investor who turns to the financial pages to study the stock market performance of various foreign countries will find a mysterious set of letters at the top of most information boxes—the EAFE Index. There are numerous indexes calculated to measure stock market performance for international investors, but the EAFE is the most prominent. Distributed by Morgan Stanley Capital International, the *EAFE index* is composed of a sample of companies representative of the market structure of 18 European and Pacific Basin countries. No nations or corporations from the Americas are represented. The index was established in 1970 and since 1972 has been computed and published on a daily basis.

The goal of the EAFE is to show the evolution of an unmanaged international portfolio, most importantly, a portfolio that as closely as possible represents the industries and the business climate of the areas covered. For example, the mix of industries in the index, 38 in all, is the same as the industry mix for the EAFE countries. Large, medium, and small capitalization stocks are included, but those companies that are dominated by a small number of shareholders are excluded.

Like all other indexes, the purpose of the EAFE is to give investors a baseline against which to measure market, share price, or portfolio performance. If the EAFE advanced 10 percent in a single year and during the same time frame an investor's international stock portfolio gained 12 percent in value, there is reason to be pleased. However, if the S&P 500 had gained 15 percent in the same year, the investor would know he should have been in U.S. stocks rather than foreign shares. If the bond index had escalated 18 percent, his money should have been in interest-bearing instruments.

Many investment advisers claim that being in the right market with the right type of investment is far more important to profits than selecting the hottest company. In other words, buying government securities when interest rates are high is likely to reap higher profits than buying the best stock available.

Investors who subscribe to this theory and who simply want to keep up with the market can buy shares in an *index fund*: the investment management company buys shares matching that of a broad-based index, such as the EAFE. The fund performance therefore mirrors that of the market as a whole. Because there is little risk and no stock-picking expertise is required to run such a fund, it is an inexpensive investment vehicle.

30

THE INTERNATIONAL STOCK EXCHANGE

The history of the securities industry in London dates back to coffeehouse trading in the mideighteenth century. Despite its venerable age, the International Stock Exchange of the United Kingdom and the Republic of Ireland (ISE) is one of the most progressive in the world. The United Kingdom radically revamped its stock exchange in 1986, the year known as the Big Bang. London opened its stock market to foreign transactions, abandoned its colorful trading floor, and adopted a version of the electronic NASDAQ system as its model. London also now resembles the United States in the detail and scope of its regulation, although its systems are still in the process of refinement. Despite these advances, the City, as London's financial center is called, has a reputation for lax accounting rules; corporate scandals occur fairly regularly. (See Key 22, Reporting Requirements.)

By virtue of tradition and geography, London is a key player in international finance and global, 24-hour trading. It was to assure the continuation of this important position in international finance that Great Britain modernized its markets. New legislation governing the stock market was adopted by Parliament in 1986 and amended in 1989, and the quasi-governmental agency that enforces the law has rewritten its rules several times since the Big Bang. Members of the securities industry have had difficulty keeping up with the frequent rule changes. Other mechanisms have been slow as well. Settlement of trades in London still takes an unusually long time, often up to two weeks.

Nevertheless, London's ISE is the third largest market in the world. It lists more than 3000 stocks and has a capitalization of more than $2.6 billion. Also associated with the ISE are six different British Isles stock exchanges, including those in Scotland, Northern Ireland, and the Republic of Ireland. Many U.S. shares are traded in London, especially by institutional investors, after North American stock exchanges have closed.

Although one of the smallest exchanges in Europe, the Irish Stock Exchange in Dublin is also one of the oldest, dating to the 1790s. In recent years it has been one of the most active, especially in regard to new issues.

In Great Britain, *ordinary shares*, as common stock is called, traditionally sell at an average price/earnings ratio of 9.6. This makes the ISE one of the cheapest markets in the industrialized world. Shares are not issued in bearer form in London, except for certain special arrangements for some internationally traded shares.

The traditional role of the United Kingdom in world trade, plus the recent expansion and modernization of its stock market, gives it a pivotal role in the European Economic Community and the rest of the world. The ISE trades the shares of many of the most important corporations in the world and is also the trading center for Great Britain's domestic companies.

Among the best-known companies in the United Kingdom are **Marks & Spencer**, British Petroleum, and **British Telecom**.

The **United Kingdom Fund** is a closed-end fund for Britain.

Jefferson Smurfit, **Allied Irish Banks**, and the **Bank of Ireland** dominate the Irish Stock Exchange. The **Irish Investment Fund** is a closed-end country fund focusing its investments on the Republic of Ireland.

(For information on the ISE indexes, see Key 31.)

31

THE FTSE INDEX

Because of the importance of the London financial community, the indicators for the International Stock Exchange are widely quoted and followed by many investors. The Financial Times Industrial Ordinary Share Index is the traditionally observed index for the ISE in London, but by no means is it the only or the most representative index. Started in 1935, the FT Ordinary Share Index is based on the shares of 30 companies considered representative of British industry and commerce. Calculated on an hourly basis, the index is a geometric, unweighted average of the 30 share prices. The index uses the base of 100 in 1962.

The newest London gauge is the Financial Times Stock Exchange 100 Shares Index. Rather than being representative of the companies that make up the entire market, the "Footsie," as it is commonly called, or FTSE 100, is based on the 100 largest capitalized stocks listed on the exchange and is calculated on a minute-by-minute basis. The FTSE 100 sister indexes often indicate something special about the markets.

The FT 500 Share Index is more broadly based, a weighted average of shares from all sectors of industry, plus oil and gas shares. The FT-Actuaries All-Share Index is the weighted, arithmetic average of the shares comprising the FT 500, plus those of financial companies, investment trusts, overseas traders, and mining finance companies. The FT-Actuaries is calculated daily and published in the *Financial Times,* which also calculates indexes for world markets. These world indexes measure market performance and year-to-date changes in local currencies and in dollars. These indexes and FT charts often are printed in the larger U.S. newspapers.

32

THE EUROPEAN ECONOMIC COMMUNITY, 1992

The year 1992 earned celebrity status as the target date for completing European unification under the umbrella of the European Community (EC). The plan is both revolutionary and ambitious. Some observers are skeptical that a unification plan will ever work among nations that share a history of scrapping, but many Europeans are enthusiastically joining in efforts to bind the continent together under more homogeneous and efficient laws, rules, and regulations. The hope is to achieve a freer, easier system of commerce and currency, leading to greater growth and prosperity and, ultimately, better investment opportunities. The driving force behind the European Community is the realization that small, insular countries have difficulty holding their own in competitive world markets. Even if the concept is only partially successful, it will have enormous significance to international investors.

The European Community is the collective designation for several European cooperative organizations including the European Economic Community also called the *Common Market*. In truth, Europe has been moving toward such unity for more than 30 years. The common market was first formed in 1957 by Belgium, France, Italy, Luxembourg, The Netherlands, and West Germany to lower trade barriers and standardize commercial practices among themselves. The concept of a barrier-free European trading area evolved until membership expanded to 12 countries, with former European dependencies in Africa and the Caribbean enjoying preferential trade status.

The EC will be the largest single market in the world. In addition to the original six countries, the EC nations also include Denmark, Ireland, Greece, Portugal, Spain, and the United Kingdom.

Austria and Sweden applied for EC membership in the early 1990s; while Finland, Norway, and Switzerland were considering seeking inclusion. Poland, Czechoslovakia, and Hungary have indicated an interest in EC membership but have been discouraged until they develop stronger economic bases. The EC is already burdened by the economic disparity of some of its members and the need for richer countries to bolster the economies of weaker neighbors.

Much attention has been given to eradicating border controls and customs red tape, but to a great extent, the success of the EC will depend on the community's ability to create and manage a common monetary system. The advantage of a central bank and single currency to the international investor would be easier currency transactions and simpler analysis of the currency risk. Rather than 12 different currencies, there will be only a single currency. A single currency is likely to be more stable than the individual country currencies and inflation more easily controlled. The success of a single currency depends on the ability of the EC to require members to curtail inflationary and other money-damaging practices. Otherwise, members with strong and stable currencies are unlikely to want their power diluted by countries with vulnerable currencies.

The European Currency Unit (ECU)—a unit devised from many currencies—is already in circulation, although not in tangible form. It is used as a measure of certain financial transactions and as an electronic transfer currency for limited utilization.

Many European stock exchanges are rapidly refiguring their stock market practices and securities laws to "harmonize" with EC standards. Furthermore, leaders of the EC have signed an agreement with the U.S. Securities and Exchange Commission to swap information and develop a more smoothly working securities system between the EC and the United States. Again, this simplification means that investors need comprehend the mechanics of only one market rather than many.

The full impact of a unified Europe will take decades to understand, although some changes have already occurred. The alliance has shown the ability to influence non-EC members in Europe, partly on the basis of size and partly because nonmember countries are beginning to see the advantages of membership. For example, under pressure from both the United States and the EC, Switzerland has removed some of the secrecy surrounding its banks, making it more difficult for dictators, drug dealers, and arms smugglers to hide their ill-gotten gains. Switzerland has also taken strides to allow greater foreign investment and improve shareholder rights on the Swiss stock exchanges. Formerly, outsiders were barred from holding a controlling interest in a Swiss company, and often foreign shareholders were only offered shares with no voting rights.

As this book was being written, the final bows were being tied on the EC package. Some critics disparaged the idea and political leaders in other countries were fearful that they will be excluded, but the European Economic Community seemed to have a powerful momentum.

33

EUROPEAN EXCHANGES

"Europhoria" swept the world in 1990 as the European Community moved toward the target date of 1992 for creating a continent without commercial barriers. Political transfiguration in Eastern Europe added to the excitement, and these developments smelled of economic opportunity. The high level of emotion eventually abated, and European stock markets lost momentum. Many international investors became disillusioned. This episode simply serves as a reminder that buying stocks or making any investment on a wave of emotion is invariably dangerous. Nevertheless, Europe remains a fertile field for international investors who study market cycles, carefully evaluate the value of corporations, and understand the nature of the separate markets. U.S. investors often feel comfortable with European markets, since North America and Europe share a common cultural heritage.

This has not meant that all European countries have welcomed foreign investment. Sweden, Spain, and Italy have had few outside investors because of their market structures, and the Swiss, with their international reputation, frequently allowed outsiders to buy only secondary shares with no voting rights. The supervisory bodies of both these countries, however, have been forced to rethink their position in light of the internationalization of securities markets.

There are active stock exchanges in Austria, Belgium, Denmark, Finland, France, Germany, Greece, Italy, Luxembourg, The Netherlands, Norway, Portugal, Spain, Sweden, Switzerland, and Turkey. London (See Key 30) boasts the third largest stock market in the world,

Germany the fourth, and France the fifth. Briefly, the major European markets look like this:

- Belgium has one of the smaller stock markets in Western Europe. There are four exchanges in the country, but Brussels does 90 percent of all transactions. The Brussels Stock Exchange recently introduced a computerized trading system and longer trading hours.
- France has the largest number of individual shareholders in Europe, and like its neighbors, the French exchanges are becoming computerized and the systems streamlined. There are seven exchanges in France, with Paris by far the leader. The Paris Stock Exchange is best known for the diversity of the companies listed there.
- German stock markets resemble Japan in that banks play an essential role. In Germany, the banks not only trade for their own accounts, they also act as underwriters, investment advisers, and brokers for private and institutional investors. Frankfurt does 70 percent of all share trading and Dusseldorf 20 percent, and the remainder is divided among six other exchanges. Shares of German companies must be bought on a foreign exchange since there are no German ADR stocks. German companies do not use U.S. accounting procedures and do not report earnings quarterly.
- Italy has been slow to embrace globalization. Not until 1989 were foreign companies able to list on the Milan exchange. Reforms began moving quickly in the late 1980s as Italy prepared for the 1992 EC deadline. The Milan Stock Exchange is the most important in Italy; there are also marts in Rome and most other major cities.
- The Netherlands holds the record for the oldest established stock exchange in existence. The United East India Company was the first company to be capitalized on the Amsterdam Stock Exchange in the seventeenth century. The ASE is the only exchange in the country, and in recent years it has grown vigorously.
- Spain's markets are dominated by banks, and liquidity until recently was sparse since shareholdings were con-

centrated in the hands of institutions and individuals with large shareholdings. The markets have opened somewhat and reforms are underway. There are exchanges in Madrid, Barcelona, Bilbao, and Valencia.

• Sweden's tight regulation and high tax rates drove many foreign investors away from the Stockholm Stock Exchange. However, numerous controls were lifted beginning in 1989, and Sweden's tax system is being radically reorganized. The markets responded positively to the news.

• Switzerland has exchanges in Zurich, Geneva, and Basel, with Zurich conducting 70 percent of all business. Nestlé, S.A. sent shock waves through the country when it departed from the Swiss tradition of a secondary class of stock for foreigners and made all its shares available to investors everywhere. Few other companies have yet to follow suit.

The European markets are undergoing enormous change as the 12 European Community member nations work toward bringing down trade and investment barriers. The EC "harmonization" program is attempting to set uniform securities rules among the member states covering such issues as settlement times and disclosure of trades. (For more on the European Community, see Key 32.) It is expected that by the end of the decade even European companies not domiciled in EC countries will comply with EC or even higher standards of reporting. By doing so the companies will be able to trade in the largest markets and attract the best investors.

However, cautious investors in Europe should limit business to established brokerage houses, mutual funds, and well-known companies. Despite a long history of securities dealing, fraud is as common on European exchanges as it is in other countries. Boiler room operations are run from those countries with limited regulatory supervision. In recent years, scandal has swept the Italian, French, German, and several other exchanges.

Among the most best-known European shares are Daimler-Benz, Deutsche Bank, and **Siemens** in Germany; Nestlé and Ciba-Geigy in Switzerland; **Unilever** in the Netherlands; **Paribas**, **Louis Vuitton** and **Compagnie Generale D'Electricite** in France; and **Telefonica de España** in Spain.

For those looking for ease in investing, many European shares can be purchased on U.S. exchanges via American Depository Receipts (See Key 9 for more information.)

Among the closed-end funds are the **Austria Fund**, the Europe Fund, the Germany Fund, the **Italy Fund**, the Spain Fund, and the Swiss Helvetia Fund.

Some selected open-ended funds are:

U.S. Services U.S. European Equity Fund (800) 873-8637

Shearson Lehman Brothers European Portfolio (800) 334-4636 or (800) 422-0214

Fidelity Europe Fund (800) 544-8888 Massachusetts only (800) 523-1919

34

THE CANADIAN EXCHANGES

The Canadian stock market is the most accessible foreign market for U.S. investors:
- We share a long border.
- In most cases (except in Quebec) business is conducted in English.
- The fundamentals of buying and selling stocks are similar.
- Many Canadian companies are listed directly on U.S. exchanges.
- Even when they are not, Canadian laws and taxes treat outside investors kindly.

Foreign investment has been important to Canada's economic development and stability, and it is estimated that about 56 percent of its manufacturing industries and 75 percent of its petroleum industry are foreign controlled. Of that investment, about three-fourths flows north from the United States. Nonresidents are subject only to some limitations to the percentage of shares they may hold in banks, certain Canadian oil and gas companies, broadcasting companies, and publicly held Ontario investment dealers.

Additionally, the Canadian markets are sophisticated and well-developed. They form the sixth largest market in the world in terms of capitalization and fourth largest when measured by volume. Some individual Canadian shares move at their own pace, but the Canadian indexes often perform similarly to the U.S. stock market indexes, although sometimes the Canadian market moves ahead of or behind that in the United States. The difference in pace may be accounted for by the heavy influence in

Canada of natural resource stocks, especially mining and lumber. Despite the prominence of natural resources, the largest and most active stocks on the Toronto and Montreal exchanges include communications, banks, utilities, and diversified companies.

There are three major exchanges in Canada: the Montreal Exchange (ME), the Toronto Stock Exchange (TSE), and the Vancouver Stock Exchange (VSE). Each province regulates its own exchange. There are small regional exchanges in Winnipeg and Calgary and an active over-the-counter market in Toronto. Montreal and Toronto are the major exchanges for senior shares. Virtually all Canadian corporations of significant size are listed on both, but each also has a diversified list of regional companies.

- The Toronto Stock Exchange is the largest in Canada, accounting for about 77 percent of the value of all shares traded. Trading hours for stocks on the TSE coincide with trading hours on the New York Stock Exchange. Like other Canadian exchanges, the TSE trades three categories of equities: common, preferred, and restricted shares. Trades are usually settled after the fifth day of business.

- Montreal, although it is older than Toronto, generates only 19 percent of the trading. With modernization, new products, and innovative links with foreign exchanges, Montreal has been the fastest growing Canadian market in the past decade.

- The Vancouver Stock Exchange is a lesser known trading arena even in Canada, yet it has earned notoriety. VSE is a venture capital market, home to hundreds of highly speculative penny stocks. It accounts for about four percent of the value of all traded shares. In the past decade, U.S. companies that face difficulty going public in the United States have used the VSE to raise capital.

Canadians often view the activities of companies listed on the Vancouver Stock Exchange (plus those of small or new issues of gas, oil, or mining shares listed on all

Canadian exchanges) with circumspection. They are likely to be wildcat ventures and subject to erratic and unpredictable action.

Avoid Canadian penny stock or any issues sold over the telephone. It is nearly impossible to verify the integrity of the promoters or the legitimacy of their claims.

However, many trustworthy corporations are based in Canada. Among the best known are **Seagram**, a liquor manufacturer with diversified holdings, **Northern Telecom**, a global communications operation, and **Canadian Pacific**, a diversified company with railroads, real estate, and involvement in almost all aspects of the Canadian economy. These and many other Canadian shares trade not only in Canada but on U.S. stock exchanges as well. (See Appendix A, New York Stock Exchange Foreign Shares.)

Although there are no closed-end country funds for Canada, there are a number of open-end mutual funds with a Canadian emphasis, including

Alliance Global, Canadian Fund, (800) 221-5672
Fidelity Canada Fund, (800) 523-1919
Mackenzie Canada, (800) 456-5111

35

THE TSE AND CANADIAN INDEXES

The most familiar indicator for the Canadian markets is the Toronto Stock Exchange Composite Index. It is also the most reflective of Canadian markets, since in terms of value, about 77 percent of Canadian shares are traded on the Toronto Stock Exchange. Introduced by the TSE in 1977, it is also called the TSE 300 because it is calculated from the capital weighted average share price of 300 of the 1208 shares listed on the TSE. The TSE Composite uses a base of 1975 = 1000. The shares included in the index are divided by the base and multiplied by 1000.

The Montreal Exchange uses the Canadian Market Portfolio Index (XXM), comprised of 25 of its most heavily capitalized stocks. The ME also publishes six subindexes covering banks, oils, utilities, forest products, industrials, and mines and metals.

The TSE and other foreign market indexes are informative since on a daily basis they show local market activity, not adjusted for currency fluctuations in relation to the U.S. dollar. Frequently, however, financial publications publish charts of various market indicators translated into the U.S. dollar. By comparing the two figures the investor is easily able to estimate the influence of currency changes on the performance of an investment.

When comparing the TSE to the Dow-Jones Industrial Average or any other index, remember that they are not directly comparable because of the differences in the represented stocks and in the way the numbers are calculated. This also applies to other U.S. and foreign stock market indicators.

The currency issue only comes into play when an investor receives dividends or when she plans to buy or sell shares. However, the fluctuations and the general direction of each of the indexes is worth checking on a regular basis: they show the prevalent trend of the·markets they cover and provide a baseline against which to compare investments within a given time frame.

36

THE AUSTRALIA AND NEW ZEALAND EXCHANGES

Australia is a long way from the United States, Europe, and Japan, and this makes it an outback market, but it also gives Australia a key position in the process of continual share trading. Markets there open after New York closes and before Tokyo or Singapore open. During the late 1980s, there were financial scandals involving some of Australia's leading corporations. Many foreign investors began avoiding the market for fear that the Australian government was not adequately supervising the management of its public companies. In efforts to reaffirm faith in the markets, however, the government has strengthened its securities watchdog agency. The Australian exchanges are also expected to stiffen financial reporting and disclosure rules for listed companies.

A relatively large market in the Pacific region, Australian exchanges rank eleventh in the world in terms of capitalization. There are electronically linked stock exchanges in each of Australia's six states, located in Adelaide, Brisbane, Hobart, Melbourne, Perth, and Sydney. Melbourne and Sydney account for about 90 percent of all trading.

Beginning in the mid-1980s, the Australian government began easing controls on foreign investment and easing outside participation in the stock markets. Because Australia is rich in minerals, oil, and other natural resources, about one-third of the listed stocks are mining or commodity shares. There is no over-the-counter market in Australia, but the Melbourne Stock Exchange Second Board Market allows small, unlisted companies access to capital.

The All-Ordinaries Index covers each of the Australian markets and is calculated on a weighted basis using 250 industrial and natural resource companies.

Broken Hill Properties, a mining concern, is the largest company listed on the Sydney Exchange. It heads a lengthy roll of Australian American Depository Receipt stocks. Also listed in the United States via ADRs are **The News Corporation, Ltd**. and **Brierley Investments, Ltd.** There is an Australia closed-end country fund, but many mutual funds for Australia are regional funds specializing in the Pacific Basin.

New Zealand has only one stock exchange, although it has trading floors in Auckland, Wellington, and Christchurch. Foreign investment in New Zealand stocks does not require regulatory permission, as long as the shareholding does not exceed 25 percent of any class of share issued by a company.

Because the New Zealand equities market is small, the most progressive companies have linked themselves to other exchanges. In one case, a down under stock issuer succeeded by knowing how to operate on both local and foreign marts. In the summer of 1991, one of the most active listings on the New York Stock Exchange was the Telecom Corporation of New Zealand, that country's recently privatized telephone company. For Telecom's sophisticated and well-planned debut on the NYSE, the New Zealand Stock Exchange was also open for trading the shares. This meant that New Zealand had to open at 1:30 A.M. to coincide with the New York opening. In New Zealand, Telecom Corporation sold for about US$2 per share, reflecting the market's taste for low-priced shares. To avoid the appearance of a penny stock in the United States, the Telecom ADR was made up of 20 shares. Telecom was well-received by U.S. investors, opening 14 percent above the offering price.

Barclay's Industrial Index is the most widely used New Zealand index. It is calculated on a weighted basis using 40 major companies. Brierley Investments, Ltd., which is also listed in Australia and in the United States via ADR, is New Zealand's largest listed company. Aside from ADR shares, the most effective way to invest in New Zealand is through Pacific regional funds.

Some established Pacific Basin funds are

Financial Strategic Portfolios, Inc., **Pacific Basin Portfolio**, (800) 525-8085

Merrill Lynch Pacific Fund, (800) 637-3863

37

THE MEXICAN BOLSA

In the 1980s, Bolsa Mexicana de Valores turned in a performance as sparkling as the glass pyramid in which it is housed. Between 1982 and 1990, the Mexico City-based exchange rose 30-fold in value. In 1991, it advanced another 78 percent, making it the world's star performer. The market's surge was based on an inflow of foreign investment, which reached $10 billion in 1990. Foreign investors account for about 28 percent of the market's capitalization and 20 percent of all trades.

The enthusiasm for Mexican investments has been the result of President Salinas de Gotardi's aggressive campaign to open the economy to global business and push a Pan-American trade agreement. The true test of Mexico's ability to modernize its economy will come under future presidencies.

A highly centralized country, Mexico has only one stock exchange of importance to foreign investors. About 200 companies are listed on the exchange, but only about 30 are actively traded. To combat fraud and investor abuse, the Mexican government in recent years has vested more regulatory power in the Ministry of Finance and Public Credit and the Mexican Securities Commission (MSC), the agencies that supervise the market.

The Mexican Bolsa has been a gold mine for investors in the past decade, but it was not without risk. The market has a history of volatility, and although the economy is improving, there are still problems. Between January and September 1987, the Mexican indicators advanced 629 percent in terms of local currency. When the October crash came, the Mexico City exchange was brutalized.

Mexico's inflation rate, at 20 percent in 1991, is still stubbornly high and a large proportion of the country's population live in poverty. Mexico's ambitions for economic development are materializing, but improved living conditions for the majority of Mexicans are slow to come.

Direct investment in the Mexican stock exchange is relatively easy to carry out. In recent years a new investment vehicle for foreigners has been offered, *debt-equity swaps*. This investment instrument trades foreign debt for corporate equity, thus alleviating Mexico of some of its oppressive debt obligation and also giving relief to international banks that carry the debt. As a result, **Grupo Industrial Alfa (Alpha Group)**, one of Mexico's largest industrial conglomerates, is now 45 percent foreign owned. Under recent changes in Mexican law, foreigners may now hold 100 percent ownership in certain Mexican companies.

Mexican companies typically offer two types of shares. Series A shares may legally be held only by Mexican citizens; Series B may also be owned by foreign investors. No special government authorization is needed to buy Series B shares. The shareholdings of institutional and other investor groups are held confidentially in Mexico, so no information is available on group holdings.

There are two types of settlements for share purchase: (1) spot or cash purchases are settled by the second business day following the trade, and (2) forward settlements may be made anytime within 360 days following the transaction, provided buyer and seller agree. Most clearing of transfers is now done by an electronic system called *Indeval,* which also provides custodial service for the shares.

Among the best known stocks on the Bolsa are **Cementos Mexicanos (Cemex)**, a cement company; **Tubos de Aceros de Mexico**, a steel company that produces pipes for the oil industry; and **Telefonos de Mexico (Telmex)**, a recently denationalized telephone company. Telmex was Latin America's biggest single privatization when the government took it public.

Numerous Mexican ADR stocks are available, including Telmex, **IEM (Industria Electrica de Mexico)**, and **International de Ceramica.**

Country funds for Mexico include the **Mexico Fund**, the **Emerging Mexico Fund**, and the Mexico Equity and Income Fund.

38

EASTERN EUROPE

The markets of Eastern Europe and the former Soviet bloc countries, with large populations frustrated by a lack of economic energy and few consumer goods, offer enormous potential markets for business and investors. There is also significant risk. Property and ownership rights remain poorly defined, communications technology is limited, market mechanisms are immature and untested, and there are serious regulatory uncertainties. However, great enthusiasm and energy seem to be directed at solving these problems. Reforms are everywhere.

- The Budapest Stock Exchange opened in 1990 with no government limit on foreign investment. Few companies trade on the exchange, but the Hungarian government plans to privatize many ventures in the first half of the 1990s.
- In 1991, the Warsaw Stock Exchange resumed trading for the first time since World War II. The only shares traded at the beginning were those of five state-run ventures that had been privatized—a glassworks, a construction firm, an electronics factory, a wire and cable manufacturer, and a clothing company. Poland intends to privatize more government-operated companies in the future and is hopeful that foreign investors will bring more capital to the domestic market.
- Romania and Czechoslovakia are exploring free-market systems and have prepared many state enterprises for sale.
- Mongolia intends to auction off state property, has built a stock exchange, and plans to make its currency convertible as soon as possible.

In most cases, the privatized entities are being sold to established corporations or placed in the hands of local citizens only. Investments in most of the former USSR Soviet bloc countries will continue to be extremely difficult until stable, convertible currencies are established. Lithuania and Ukraine have created their own new currencies, but it will be some time before the status of the ruble is fully understood or the new money is tested and deemed reliable.

Several regional funds have been set up for Eastern Europe, but in the early 1990s most were holding the majority of their capital in cash. In the near term the best access to Eastern European markets is through public corporations that have entered those markets independently, have purchased state-owned factories, or have established joint ventures with Eastern European partners. There are many such corporations, among them the Coca Cola Company, the Fiat Group, General Motors, and several multinational oil companies, including Exxon.

39

HONG KONG AND NEIGHBORING EXCHANGES

Measured in U.S. dollars, the Hong Kong Stock Exchange pressed forward by 40.4 percent in 1991, compared to a 23.8 percent escalation in U.S. stock markets.

There is considerable nervousness over what will transpire in Hong Kong after China reclaims its territory in 1997. Nobody knows for sure what changes will take place, but Hong Kong's ties to China and its huge, untapped consumer market may very well turn out to be an asset.

The Hang Seng Index is the main indicator for the Hong Kong exchange. It is made up of 33 companies and is heavily influenced by large capitalization stocks.

Despite their aggressive economies, some of the Four Dragons have discouraged equity investment. Korea and Taiwan, for example, until recently restricted most foreign investment to country funds. Beginning in 1992, foreigners can invest directly in Korean stocks, and Taiwan is close to changing its policies.

In Singapore, the majority of investors have traditionally been foreigners. Singapore now operates on a computerized basis, and the system is linked to the National Association of Securities Dealers (NASD) trading system in the United States to allow access to U.S. and European stocks. The Singapore stock market rose 20.9 percent in 1991, measured in U.S. dollars.

There is a wide selection of funds and ADR stocks for Hong Kong, Singapore, and the Pacific region in general. The Korea Fund, ROC Taiwan Fund, and Singapore Fund are closed-end and trade on the New York Stock Exchange. "Tiger" funds, often open-end and listed with the mutual funds, are those that specialize in Hong Kong, Singapore, Malaysia, Korea, and Taiwan.

40

OTHER ASIAN MARKETS

Indonesia, Malaysia, the Philippines, Thailand, and China have captured investor imagination, especially as their larger neighbors move from economies based on cheap labor to the production and control of their own technologies. The emerging dragons welcome foreign investment and in recent years have lowered barriers to outside participation.

- Although political turmoil has heightened investment risk in Indonesia, an ever-increasing number of companies have listed on the Jakarta Stock Exchange and investment has been strong. At the beginning of 1989 only 24 stocks were listed on the Jakarta exchange. By the end of 1990 there were 150.
- Malaysia's Kuala Lumpur Stock Exchange became a favorite with foreign investors in the late 1980s, and in 1990 split itself off from the Stock Exchange of Singapore. Malaysia's economy has been restructured in recent years away from dependence on oil. Growth has fueled concern over inflation, but Malaysia enjoys a stable government.
- The markets in the Philippines, dominated by metal and crude oil stocks, have gained strength since the Marcos government was deposed. Shares on Philippine exchanges are divided into two classes, Big Board and Small Board stocks. The speculative shares of companies that have not yet launched operation, mainly mining exploration companies, are restricted to the Small Board.
- Thailand has been one of the liveliest emerging exchanges in the world. However, an unsettled political atmosphere has sometimes been its undoing.

- Economic reform has begun in China, yet there remain long-term concerns about the country's political leadership and economic policies following the 1989 riots at Tiananmen Square. The concept of shareholder-owned companies is evolving, although the actual number of publicly traded companies is small. Shenzhen, Shanghai, and Beijing have fledgling exchanges.

There are few funds with direct investments in China and no ADR stocks. Despite the emergence of exchanges, the simplest way to invest in China is through companies that trade on the Hong Kong exchange and do business in China, or through multinational corporations involved in joint ventures or other forms of business in China.

There is a good selection of Malaysia listed ADR stocks, only one from the Philippines, and none from Indonesia. There are no listed ADR stocks from Thailand, but there are several Thai closed-end country funds.

The Indonesia Fund, **Jakarta Fund**, Malaysia Fund, and **First Philippines Fund** are closed-end and trade on the New York Stock Exchange. Tiger funds are regional funds that specialize in Hong Kong, Singapore, Malaysia, Korea, and Taiwan.

Among the open-end mutual funds are:

G.T. Pacific Growth Fund, (800) 824-1580

T. Rowe Price New Asia Fund, (800) 638-5660

41

SOUTH AMERICAN MARKETS

Few entitles have blazed onto stage with the verve of the Latin American stock markets. Entering the 1990s, Mexico took the limelight, but investor interest also extended south to Argentina, Brazil, Chile, Venezuela, and Uruguay.

Many South American countries have been working toward freer economies with the hope of attracting outside investors. If a proposed free-trade alliance encompassing all three Americas becomes a reality, all of Latin America is expected to prosper. Even now, however, changes are apparent. In 1991, every South American country except Brazil and Peru showed growth in gross regional product. Some economists see South America as a more promising investment arena than China, Eastern Europe, or Russia because the region has more experience with capitalism. Even so, some structural and political barriers to investment remain.

• Chile has been especially successful in curbing inflation and attracting foreign investment. The fastest growing Latin American country in the last half of the 1980s, Chile has reformed its economy and modernized its markets. Much foreign investment was attracted through debt-equity swaps and mutual funds. A privatization program completed in 1989 involving 33 state-owned industries, greatly increased the volume of business in the Chilean equity markets. Accounting procedures and disclosure requirements for public companies have been vastly improved and the stock exchange computerized, which automates settlements and transfers as well. There are stock exchanges in

Santiago and Valparaiso, with Santiago handling by far the majority of the trade.

- Brazil has staggered under oppressive debt and has attempted economic reforms, yet public sentiment has run against privatization of public assets as a solution. There are 10 stock exchanges in the country, with São Paulo and Rio de Janeíro the two most important. Brazil has taken steps toward modernizing its system by linking its exchanges electronically and establishing a total market index, but the market needs additional tax and other changes. Because of regulations restricting the entry and recovery of capital, investment in Brazil is mostly limited to a few country and regional funds.

- The stock exchange in Buenos Aires was founded in 1854 and is the oldest in Latin America. Like so many other Latin American countries, trading in Argentina is dominated by government securities; the few equities trading there are controlled by a small number of shareholders, often family groups. The largest obstacle for foreign investors is Argentina's political uncertainty. Argentina has been plagued by inflation and currency instability, but in 1991 its stock market surged 112 percent when the government announced that the austral would be fully convertible to dollars.

- In 1990, the Venezuelan government eliminated restrictions against foreign investment in its stock markets and liberalization of taxes on investment income is being considered, although foreign investors are still likely to find regulatory conditions challenging, since only from the end of the 1980s has the country attempted to draw foreign investors. The Caracas Stock Exchange is the leading market, and in 1986 a new exchange was formed in Maracaibo.

- Uruguay is considered a relatively safe and stable haven for money by other South Americans, and it has liberal and progressive investment rules. Its only market, Montevideo, is tiny and consists mainly of government securities.

- The remaining Latin American countries either have no stock exchanges or, like Ecuador and Peru, the exchanges are too small or too restricted to be accessible to most investors. An exception is El Salvador's **Compania de Alumbrado Electrico de San Salvador**, which trades over-the-counter via ADR.

Latin America is undergoing rapid change, but individual investors will still find it somewhat complicated to participate in equity markets there, except through international and global funds. As yet, there are no exchange-listed Argentinian, Brazilian, Chilean, Venezuelan, or Uruguayan ADR stocks.

Investments can be made through the closed-end Latin America Fund and **Latin America Equity Fund**. There are closed-end country funds for Argentina, Brazil, and Chile, and because new country and regional funds are being formed on a regular basis, other countries are also likely to be covered eventually.

42

THE
JOHANNESBURG
STOCK EXCHANGE

In the summer of 1991, the United States lifted political sanctions against the Republic of South Africa because of that country's progress in ending apartheid, making it again acceptable for U.S. citizens to invest in the Johannesburg Stock Exchange (JSE). Immediately there was a surge of interest in South African issues. Even when formal sanctions ceased, however, many pension funds and other institutional investors were prohibited by their governing boards from buying shares of companies with financial ties to South Africa.

Investment interest, as has always been the case, has focused on South Africa's gold mines. South Africa is a large and diverse country, and mineral wealth underpins the economy. In addition to gold, South Africa has massive reserves of platinum, coal, manganese, vanadium, and chrome. Mining companies represent 55 percent of the value of the JSE, which is the only exchange in the country.

Subordinated to the JSE are the Development Capital Market (DCM), which is open to companies that cannot meet the big board requirements, and the Venture Capital Market, where venture capital companies can be listed.

The JSE Actuaries Indices reflects the performance of the South African market, although it is constructed to reflect the performance of larger companies. It is believed the larger corporations have a disproportionate impact on the economy. Share prices of gold stocks, as expected, have an extraordinary ability to move the market. Gold prices, and hence gold shares, are extremely sensitive to the South African rand/U.S. dollar exchange rate. When the rand weakens against the dollar, gold prices are likely to surge, and vice versa.

Some typical shares trading on the JSE are **Anglo American Corporation of South Africa, Lonrho**, and **De Beers Consolidated Mines**. Nearly 100 South African American Depositary Receipt stocks trade in the U.S. markets.

No open-end mutual funds are focused on South Africa, but shares of companies from this country can be found in precious metal, gold, or natural resource funds. (For more information, see Key 43, Mining Stocks.)

43

MINING STOCKS

Important mining companies produce such metals as coal, tin, iron, copper, titanium, aluminum, and silver, but the mining shares that absorb the most attention are gold shares. Some stock markets trace their origins to the formation of mining corporations, and metal shares continue to heavily influence these markets. These countries include Argentina, Australia, Canada, South Africa, and the Philippines.

The price of all mining shares follows the performance of the underlying metal in the commodity and commodities futures markets. The commodity price depends, of course, on supply, demand, and anticipated supply and demand for the product.

A gold investment can take three forms: hard metal in the form of coins or bullion, mining shares, or mutual funds.

The market price of gold coins and *bullion* (bulk metal, often bars or ingots) follow the same principle, but gold, because of its unique properties, is also frequently seen as a proxy for confidence in the world economy.

- Gold shares bring an added dimension to pricing. The shares represent not only the actual quality, quantity, and demand for the assets (gold) behind the shares but also the management ability of the company and the cost of production. Although they carry an added element of risk, gold shares and gold funds are simpler to buy, hold, store, and sell than actual gold coins or bullion. Unlike gold itself, gold shares frequently pay dividends. Because gold shares are quoted on several different stock exchanges, they are a frequent object of arbitrage play. (For more information on arbitrage, read Key 24.)

- Silver has been a popular metal in the past, and historically, silver prices move in tandem with gold prices though at a lower level. The relationship between gold and silver has eroded in recent years, however, and silver prices have been unusually depressed. Mexico is a major silver producer, but the stock market there has diversified well beyond any dependence on silver.
- Copper is another important industrial metal; there are several international stocks in this sector. **Zambia Consolidated Copper Mines, Ltd.** and **Mhangura Copper Mines, Ltd.** of Zimbabwe trade in over-the-counter ADRs.

When contemplating mining stocks, it is wise to take a cue from Canadian investors. Canadians have long understood the speculative nature of mining shares, and gold in particular, on the stock exchange. They approach new companies, especially those created within the corporate "shell" of an inoperative company, with a "buyer beware" attitude. Too many of these companies have been used to raise cash for extremely dubious exploration and development and have lasted only a short time. The attitude of Canadian investors on apparently speculative mining shares is that timing may be more important than value. Get in when the shares are new and prices are rising, and sell before the organizers suddenly dispose of their own shares and allow the share price to collapse. Despite the industry's shady history, some mining companies have long records of operation and have served investors well.

Mining stocks are well-represented by American Depository Receipts. The keys covering Canada (Key 34), South Africa (Key 42), and other prominent metal-producing countries give more information on direct investments. Some of the most active gold stocks are Anglo-American Corporation and **Kloof** in South Africa, **Placer Dome** in Canada, and Broken Hill Proprietary Company in Australia.

Several funds specialize in mining and precious metals shares: **Kemper Gold Fund**, (800) 621-1148; **Franklin Gold Fund**, (800) 632-2350; **Vanguard Gold and Precious Metals Portfolio**, (800) 662-7447

44

OTHER STOCK MARKETS

It is possible to participate in stock markets in the most exotic reaches of the world, although it is not always easy to do so. Information becomes increasingly sketchy with decreasing size of the markets. Liquidity is limited on markets with low trading volumes, making it harder to buy or sell shares at will. Overall, risk increases as trading venues become more obscure. However, the unknown markets of today may well be the emerging markets of tomorrow. They cannot be ignored.

- The Tel Aviv Stock Exchange (TASE) is one of the best developed capital markets in the Middle East, and numerous Israeli ADRs trade on U.S. exchanges. Israel has steadily developed high-technology prowess, and many of the stocks traded represent this sector of the market. TASE is dominated by mutual funds, with direct foreign investment relatively low. This may change as the Israeli government enacts plans to sell off state-owned companies. Some Israeli ADR stocks are **Bank Leumi Le-Israel** and **IDB Bankholding Corporation**.

- The Kuwait Stock Exchange is characteristic of many Middle Eastern exchanges that suffer from excessive speculation and lack of regulation. The Kuwait exchange was formally established in 1977, and it, along with a parallel over-the-counter market known as the *Soukh al Manakh*, rose very quickly. Then in 1982 prices suddenly collapsed, requiring government intervention. Now most shares are controlled by the government. The Kuwait-Iraq war of 1991 understandably interrupted plans for an electronic trading system.

- During the oil boom of the 1970s and 1980s, Nigeria's

stock market was viewed as one of the most important emerging markets in the world. When oil became plentiful, however, investors slipped away from the Nigerian market. The government in recent years has undertaken privatization and other reforms to public enterprises, but international investors have been slow to return. Nigeria is expected to move from a military-controlled to a civilian government in 1992, and if political stability is restored, investors may again find this one of the few attractive emerging markets in Africa.

- For decades, participation in India's economy was reserved for Indian citizens and persons of Indian origin. However, starting in the early 1990s, India took steps to encourage foreign investment. India has tried several times to reform its protective economy, so investors are taking a wait-and-see attitude on the most recent attempts. There are no ADR stocks from India; investment is best accomplished through mutual funds, such as the **India Fund** or the **India Growth Fund.**

- Most of the shares trading on Pakistan's Karachi Stock Exchange represent offshoots of multinational corporations primarily owned by a few wealthy Pakistani families. Plans were underway for a massive expansion of the exchange, but the country has been plagued by political unrest. The long-term outlook is a mystery.

- There are three stock exchanges in the Caribbean—Jamaica, Barbados, and a third combined mart for Trinidad and Tobago. All are lilliputian and subject to shifting economic and political temperaments. In recognition of the importance of regional alliances, however, plans are underway to meld the three exchanges into an unified stock market. There are several ADR stocks of Bermuda-based companies, including **BT Shipping** and **Jardine, Matheson Holdings, Ltd.**

A number of global and international funds invest in the shares of emerging markets. They are seeking growth but are relying on their wide diversification to protect them from the heightened risks. Two such funds are **IDS Global Growth Fund**, (800) 328-8300 and **European Emerging Companies Fund**, (800) 323-USGF.

45

U.S. SOURCES OF INFORMATION

Steadfast international investors cull information from a profusion of sources. They are information detectives, and, as such, discover that global investment practices are being rapidly refined and much outdated or conflicting information is afloat. Most difficult of all, some information is colored by cultural views, societal differences, or the calculated misdirections of someone bent on selling a particular investment. The only defense is to turn to the most trustworthy, objective sources of facts available and try to check every bit of key information twice.

The following data sources are listed in Key 46, and although sources named there are published abroad, they are frequently available in the United States.

- Among the general daily newspapers, *The Wall Street Journal, Investors Daily,* and the *New York Times* are of the greatest use to the international stock investor. These newspapers have a dedication to world news and enough space to print the essential stories.
- On a weekly basis, *Barron's* and *BusinessWeek* offer extensive charts, tables, and news analysis.
- *Forbes, Fortune,* and the monthly business magazines tend to be more colorful and "newsy" in their presentation, but they publish detailed corporate profiles and are helpful in keeping up with global trends.

The Complete ADR Directory is published annually by The Bank of New York. It identifies and describes each American Depository Receipt issue that trades regardless of the depository bank. For information about the directory, contact The Bank of New York, ADR Division, 101 Barclay Street, New York, NY 10286, (212) 815-2294.

Emerging Stock Markets Factbook 1990 is available from International Finance Corporation, a World Bank affiliate charged with the responsibility of promoting investments in emerging stock markets. The telephone number is (202) 473-9110.

The Directory of Multinationals, published by Macmillan, gives excellent corporate histories and includes basic financial information. *Diamond's Japan Business Directory* is a valuable resource for Japanese corporations.

Value Line Investment Survey prints detailed financial information on U.S. and foreign stocks, as well as closed-end country funds. The service is available in many public and brokerage libraries. A subscription costs $495 a year. The address for Value Line is 711 Third Avenue, New York, NY 10017.

Standard & Poor's Corporate registry also provides investment information on some foreign corporations. These reports and other S&P information often are provided by a broker and are found in the reference sections of most public libraries. For more details, contact Standard & Poor's Corporation, 25 Broadway, New York, NY 10004, (800) 221-5277.

Comprehensive investment information based on institutional reports is available through the mail or by computer modem from *Investext,* Thomson Financial Networks, 11 Farnsworth Street, 4th Floor, Boston, MA 02210, (800) 662-7878. The cost depends on the level of service and number of reports requested.

46

FOREIGN SOURCES OF INFORMATION

There are many news and information resources from abroad for international investors, although most take extra effort to find. The cost is sometimes higher than most individual investors are willing to pay. Fortunately, nearly all the newspapers, magazines, and other publications mentioned here are available at good libraries and through some computer data bases.

Newspapers: In Europe, the *International Herald Tribune* is a leading English-language newspaper. The stories are brief, but it has more and fresher international news than most U.S. newspapers. The address is 181 Avenue Charles de Gaulle, 92200 Neuilly-Sur-Seine, France.

The *Financial Times* of London, one of the most respected international business newspapers, is now printed and delivered in the United States. The cost of the distinctive buff-colored newspaper is approximately $365 per year in the United States. For *Financial Times* subscription information, contact the FT at 14 East 60th Street, New York, NY 10023, (212) 752-4500 or (800) 628-8088.

For Japan and the Far East, *The Asian Wall Street Journal* is a well-regarded source of information. A subscription to *The Asian Wall Street Journal* runs around $225 per year. The address is 200 Liberty Street, New York, NY 10281, (212) 416-2000 or (800) 622-2743.

The Japanese daily newspaper *Asahi Shimbun* publishes a weekly news briefing from Japan called *Japan Access*, with subscription costs of $200 per year. A subscription can be requested by writing to *Japan Access*, Asahi Shimbun International, Inc., 757 Third Avenue, New York, NY 10017, (800) 666-0170.

Periodicals: The *Economist,* published in London, is both entertaining and informative. Its news covers the entire world, frequently with a startlingly different perspective from that of most U.S. publications. The magazine also contains international interest rate charts and other technical information. A one-year subscription averages $100. The U.S. address is 111 West 57th Street, New York, NY 10019.

The monthly magazine *Euromoney* provides an uncommonly thorough look at the banking industry, financial markets, and economic affairs in Europe. For U.S. subscription information, contact *Euromoney*, Reed Business Publications, 205 East 42nd Street, Suite 1705, New York, NY 10017, (212) 867-2080.

Swiss Review of World Affairs offers broad information on world political and economic developments. Published monthly in English, the cost is $48 per year. The address is Neue Zuricher Zeitung, P.O. Box 660, CH-8021 Zurich, Switzerland.

The "bible" of the professional investor, *Morgan Stanley Capital International Perspective,* is purely statistical in nature. The individual investor is well-advised to locate the service at a library or on a financial computer data base, since the cost is about $3500 annually. For those who are still interested, write Morgan Stanley Capital International, 3 Place des Bergues, CH-1201 Geneva, Switzerland.

Books and directories: The *Japan Company Handbook,* published by Toyo Keizai, Inc., gives important details of Japanese companies. It is available in the more complete business sections of public and university libraries.

One of the most useful directories is the annual *GT Guide to World Equity Markets*. It is published jointly by GT Management, an international fund management house and Euromoney Publication, p.l.c. The manual alphabetically lists each country that has an equities market and then systematically describes the market and its background, performance, types of shares, investors, tax practices, and research and reporting quality. Details are given for each exchange in a country. For information on the *GT Guide*, contact Euromoney Publications at the address given previously.

Although the stock market information is not as extensive as that in the previous manual, *The 1991 Handbook of World Stock & Commodity Exchanges* begins with a valuable series of essays on developments in world markets. It is published annually by World Ticker International, Basil Blackwell, Inc., London. It is also available at larger libraries.

47

INTERNATIONAL INVESTMENT NEWSLETTERS

There is something seductive about a stock tip. Hundreds of investment advisory letters flood the publishing market each year, and millions of investors subscribe to them at prices ranging from $50 to $1000 per year. Some letters are strictly statistical in nature; others analyze the markets or particular shares in terms of an investment philosophy or technique. A few words of warning: if you do not understand the technical or historical basis on which a tip sheet or newsletter is basing its recommendations, find another source of advice. If recommendations seem founded on intuition, emotions, or a rigid personal or religious ideology, avoid the advisory service. The best newsletters offer factually based data and interpret the information in a way that a reasonably intelligent person can grasp. Anything else is hocus-pocus.

The *Hurlbert Financial Guide* is published monthly and the *Hurlbert Guide to Financial Newsletters* is published annually in February. The guide describes each investment letter and evaluates it in terms of specific criteria. Hurlbert follows the advice of 135 newsletters and tracks their success. The author, Mark Hurlbert, also pens a monthly column for *Forbes* magazine discussing investment newsletters. The *Hurlbert Guide* can be contacted by telephoning (703) 683-5905.

Most investment letters will send a sample copy on request. Also, the Select Information Exchange provides trial subscriptions to 380 different services for a small fee, beginning at $11.95 for 20 different services. The telephone number for SIE is (212) 247-7123.

The following list is a sampling of established newsletters that track international markets, U.S. multinational corporations with extensive global investments, American Depository Receipt shares, and/or foreign stocks:

Capital International Perspective, Morgan Stanley, 1251 Avenue of the Americas, New York, NY 10020 (212) 703-2965

Dessauer's Journal of Financial Markets, P.O. Box 1718, Orleans, MA 02653 (508) 255-1651

International Fund Monitor, Research International, Inc., P.O. Box 5754, Washington, DC 20016 (202) 363-3097

Investment Quality Trends, 7440 Girard Street, Suite 4, La Jolla, CA 92037 (619) 459-3818

Investor's Guide to Closed-End Funds, Box 161465, Miami, FL 33116 (305) 271-1900

Appendix A

NEW YORK STOCK EXCHANGE FOREIGN SHARES

The New York Stock Exchange is one of the most prestigious stock markets in the world, and the companies traded there must comply with strict listing standards. The most common way for foreign companies to list their shares on the NYSE is by American Depository Receipt shares (ADRs), as described in Key 9. However, some foreign companies trading on the NYSE are headquartered in nations where regulations are similar to those in the United States. Some companies go one step further and elect to be treated exactly as U.S. stocks—for example, in terms of accounting, reporting, listing, and other requirements. In other words, these companies list their shares *directly* on the big board.

Many companies, however, do not follow accounting or reporting procedures comparable to those in the United States. NYSE listing requirements are more stringent than they are for many corporations listed in their home countries. For companies to list directly on the NYSE, the company must have cumulative pretax income for the last three years of at least $100,000,000, with a minimum of $25,000,000 in any one of the three years. In addition, net tangible assets worldwide must total at least $100,000,000; the aggregate market value of publicly held shares must total at least $100,000,000 worldwide; the number of shares publicly held must be at least 2,500,000; and finally, there must be 5000 or more shareholders owning more than 100 shares each, worldwide. For this reason, the foreign corporations trading on the NYSE represent some of the largest and best capitalized companies in the world.

The following is a list of the ADRs shares that trade on the NYSE.

Non-U.S. Companies Traded on the NYSE*
*As of November 5, 1991.

Country	Company	Symbol	ADRs
Australia			
	Broken Hill Proprietary Company, Ltd.	BHP	X
	Coles Myer, Ltd.	CM	X
	FAI Insurances, Limited	FAI	X
	National Australia Bank, Ltd.	NAB	X
	News Corporation, Ltd.	NWS	X
	Western Mining Corporation, Ltd.	WMC	X
	Westpac Banking Corporation	WBK	
Bermuda			
	ADT Limited (common & ADRs)	ADT	X
British West Indies			
	Club Med, Inc.	CMI	
Canada			
	Abitibi-Price, Inc.	ABY	
	Alcan Aluminum, Ltd.	AL	
	American Barrick Resources Corporation	ABX	
	Avalon Corporation	AVL	
	BCE, Inc.	BCE	
	Campbell Resources, Inc.	CCH	
	Canadian Pacific, Ltd.	CP	
	Cineplex Odeon Corporation	CPX	
	Curragh Resources	CZP	
	Domtar, Inc.	DTC	
	Horsham Corporation	HSM	
	Inco, Ltd.	N	
	Inter Tan, Inc.	ITN	

Inter Tan, Inc.	ITN	
LAC Minerals, Ltd.	LAC	
Laidlaw, Inc. (Class A & B)	LDW	
Mitel Corporation	MLT	
Moore Corporation	MCL	
NOVA Corporation	NVL	
Northern Telecom, Ltd.	NT	
Northgate Exploration, Ltd.	NGX	
Placer Dome, Inc.	PDQ	
Potash Corporation	POT	
Ranger Oil, Ltd.	RGO	
Seagram Company	VO	
TransCanada Pipeline	TRP	
United Dominion Industries, Ltd.	UDI	
Westcoast Energy, Inc.	WE	

Chile

Compania de Telefonos de Chile	TCH	X

Denmark

Novo-Nordisk, A/S	NVO	X

France

Rhone-Poulenc, S.A., (two issues)	RPU	X
Societe Nationale Elf Aquitaine	ELF	X
TOTAL	TOT	X

Hong Kong

Hong Kong Telecommunications, Ltd.	HKT	X
Universal Matchbox Group, Ltd.	UMG	

Ireland

Allied Irish Banks, p.l.c.	ALB	X

Israel

Elscint, Ltd.	ELT	

Italy

Benetton Group, s.p.a.	BNG	X
Fiat, s.p.a.	FIA	X
Luxottica Group, s.p.a.	LUX	X
Montedison, s.p.a.	MNT	X

Japan			
	Hitachi, Ltd.	HIT	X
	Honda Motor Company, Ltd.	HMC	X
	Kubota, Ltd.	KUB	X
	Kyocera Corporation	KYO	X
	Matsushita Electric Industrial Company	MC	X
	Pioneer Electronic Corporation	PIO	X
	Sony Corporation	SNE	X
	TDK Corporation	TDK	X
Mexico			
	Telefonos de Mexico, S.A.	TMX	X
Netherlands			
	KLM Royal Dutch Airlines	KLM	X
	Philips, N.V.	PHG	X
	Polygram, N.V.	PLG	X
	Royal Dutch Petroleum Company	RD	X
	Unilever, N.V.	UN	X
	AEGON, N.V.	AEG	X
Netherlands Antilles			
	Schlumberger, Ltd.	SLB	
	The Singer Company, N.V.	SEW	
New Zealand			
	Telecom Corporation of New Zealand, Ltd.	NZT	X
Norway			
	Norsk Hydro, s.s.	NHY	X
Philippines			
	Benquet Corporation	BE	
South Africa			
	ASA Limited	ASA	
Spain			
	Banco Bilbao Vizoaya, S.A.	BBV	X
	Banco Central, S.A.	BCM	X

	Banco de Santander	STD	X
	Empress Nacional de Electricidad, S.A.	ELE	X
	Repsol, S.A.	REP	X
	Telefonica de España, S.A.	TEF	X
United Kingdom			
	Attwoods, p.l.c.	A	X
	Barclays, p.l.c.	BCS	X
	Bass, p.l.c.	BAS	X
	Beazer, p.l.c.	BZR	X
	BET, p.l.c.	BEP	X
	British Airway, p.l.c.	BAB	X
	British Gas, p.l.c.	BRG	X
	British Petroleum, p.l.c.	BP	X
	British Steel, p.l.c.	BST	X
	British Telecommunications, p.l.c.	BTY	X
	Cable and Wireless, p.l.c.	CWP	X
	Glaxo Holdings, p.l.c.	GLX	X
	Grand Metropolitan, p.l.c.	GRM	X
	Hanson, p.l.c.	HAN	X
	Huntingdon International Holdings	HTD	X
	Imperial Chemical Industries, p.l.c.	ICI	X
	National Westminster, p.l.c.	NW	X
	Royal Bank of Scotland Group, p.l.c.	RBS	X
	RTZ Corporation, p.l.c.	RTZ	X
	Saatchi & Saatchi Company, p.l.c.	SAA	X
	"Shell" Transport and Trading Company, Ltd.	SC	X
	Smith Kline Beecham, p.l.c. (two issues)	SBH	X
	Tiphook, p.l.c.	TPH	X
	Unilever, p.l.c.	UL	X
	Vodafone Group, p.l.c.	VOD	X
	Willis Corroon, p.l.c.	WCG	X

Appendix B

MAJOR WORLD STOCK EXCHANGES

*Only includes lead exchanges in each country.

Argentina:
Mercado de Valores de Buenos Aires
25 de Mayo 367
8th & 9th Floors   Tel. 313-4522 or 313-5552
1002 Buenos Aires

Australia:
Australian Stock Exchange, Ltd.
Level 9, Plaza Building
Australia Square
Sydney, NSW 2000
Postal Address: GPO Box 520
Sydney, NSW 2001   Tel. 233-5266

Austria:
Wiener Borsekammer (Vienna Stock Exchange)
Wipplingerstrasse 34
A-1011 Vienna, Austria   Tel. 53 499

Belgium:
Bourse de Bruxelles, Beurs Van Brussel
1000 Brussels   Tel. 509-1211

Brazil:
Bolsa de Valores do Rio de Janeiro
Pca XV Novembre 20, 9th Floor
20010 Rio de Janeiro/RJ   Tel. 291-5354

Bolsa de Valores de São Paulo
Rue Alvares Penteado 151
151 São Paulo   Tel. 258-7222

Canada:
Toronto Stock Exchange
The Exchange Tower
2 First Canadian Place
Toronto, Ontario
M5X 1J2   Tel. 947-4700

The Montreal Exchange
Stock Exchange Tower
800 Victoria Square
Montreal, Quebec
H4Z 1A9   Tel. 871-2424

Vancouver Stock Exchange
Stock Exchange Tower
P.O. Box 10333
609 Graville Street
Vancouver, BC   Tel. 689-3334
V7Y 1H1

Chile:
Bolsa de Comercio de Santiago
Casilla 123-D Santiago   Tel. 698-2001

Denmark:
Kobenhavns Fondsbors
Nikolaj Plads 2
P.O. Box 1040
DK-1067 Copenhagen K   Tel. 93 36 66

Finland:
Helsingin Avropaperiporssi
Fabianinkatu 14
P.O. Box 361
SF-00131 Helsinki   Tel. 173-301

France:
Palais de la Bourse
4 Place de la Bourse
75080 Paris   Tel. 140 41 100 00

Germany:
Frankfurter Wertpapierborse
Borsenplatz 6
Postfach 10 08 11
6000 Frankfurt 1   Tel. 219371

Greece:
The Athens Stock Exchange
10 Sophocleous Street
Athens 10559   Tel. 321-1301

Hong Kong:
The Stock Exchange of Hong Kong, Ltd.
First Floor
Exchange Square
Hong Kong
P.O. Box 8888   Tel 5 22 11 22

India:
The Stock Exchange
Bombay
Phirtoze Jeejeebhoy Towers
Dalal Street
Bombay 400 023   Tel. 27 06 71 or 27 25 23

Indonesia:
Capital Market Executive Exchange
Jalan Medan Merdeka Selatan 13/14
P.O. Box 439
Jakarta   Tel. 36 14 60 or 35 55 09

Ireland:
The Irish Stock Exchange
28 Anglesea Street
Dublin 2   Tel. 77 88 08

Israel:
The Tel Aviv Stock Exchange
54 Ahad Ha'am Street
Tel Aviv   Tel. 03 62 74 11

Italy:
Borsa Valori di Milano
Piazza Degli Affari 6
20123 Milan   Tel. 2 853 446 36

Japan:
Tokyo Stock Exchange
2-1 Nihombashi-Kabuto
Chuo-ku
Tokyo 103   Tel. 666-0141

Korea:
Korea Stock Exchange
33 Yoido-dong
Youngduengpo-ku
Seoul 150-010   Tel. 780-2271

Luxembourg:
Societe de la Bourse de Luxembourg, S.A.
11 avenue de la Porte-Neuvre
BF 165
L-2011 Luxembourg   Tel. 47 79 36-1

Malaysia:
The Kuala Lumpur Stock Exchange
3rd & 4th Floors
Komplex Bukit Naga
Off Jalan Semantan
Damansara Heights
Kuala Lumpur 50490
Malaysia   Tel. 254-6433

Mexico:
Bolsa Mexicana de Valores
Uruguay, Colonia Centro 68

Delagacion Cuauhtemoc 0600
Mexico, DF   Tel. 5-510-4620

Netherlands:
Amsterdam Effectenbeurs
Beursplein 5
1012 JW Amsterdam   Tel. 20 23 97 11

New Zealand:
New Zealand Stock Exchange
8th Floor, Caltex Tower
286-292 Lambton Quay
P.O. Box 2959
Wellington   Tel. 72 75 199

Norway:
Oslo Bors
P.O. Box 460-Sentrum
0105 Oslo 1   Tel. 02 84 17 00

Philippines:
Manila Stock Exchange
Prensa St Cor Muelle de la Industria Binondo
Manila   Tel. 47 11 25 or 40 88 60

Makati Stock Exchange Building
Ayala Avenue
Metro Manila   Tel. 88 78 71 or 88 64 11

Portugal:
Bolsa de Valores de Lisboa
Rua dos Ranqueiros 10
1100 Lisboa   Tel. 87 94 16 or 87 94 17
Bolsa de Valores do Oporto
Palacio de Bolsa
4000 Oporto   Tel. 31 85 46 or 31 86 24

Singapore:
Stock Exchange of Singapore, Ltd.
1 Raffles Place, 24-00

OUB Centre
Singapore 0104   Tel. 535 378

South Africa:
The Johannesburg Stock Exchange
Diagonal Street
P.O. Box 1174
2000 Johannesburg   Tel. 833-6580

Spain:
Bolsa de Madrid
Plaza de la Lealtad 1
28014 Madrid   Tel. 1 1221 4790 or 1 221 4799

Sweden:
Stockholm Fondbors
Kallargrand 2
P.O. Box 1256
S-111 82 Stockholm   Tel. 613-8800

Switzerland:
Zurich Stock Exchange
Bleicherweg 5
CH-8021 Zurich   Tel. 299-2111

Taiwan:
Taiwan Stock Exchange Corporation
7–10th floors, City Building
85 Yen-Ping South Road
Taipei, Taiwan   Tel. 311-4020 or 396-9270

Thailand:
Securities Exchange of Thailand
Sinthon Building 2nd floor
132 Wireless Road
Bangkok 10500 Metropolis   Tel. 250-0001-8 or
250-0010-15

Turkey:
Istanbul Stock Exchange

Borsasi
Rihtim C, 254, Karakoy
Istanbul, 80030   Tel. 1-152 48 00

United Kingdom:
The International Stock Exchange
Throgmorton Street
London EC2N 1HP   Tel. 588-2355

Venezuela:
Bolsa de Valores de Caracas
Avenue Urdaneta de Santa
Santa Capilla a Carmelitas
Banco Central de Venezuela
Piso 19, Caracas   Tel. 81 51 41

QUESTIONS AND ANSWERS

Who should invest in international stocks?

Because of the globalization of business, the advanced state of many foreign economies, and the speed and efficiency of international communication—any stock portfolio without some representation by international equities is insufficiently diverse.

What percentage of my stock portfolio should be in foreign shares?

All investors need some foreign stocks, though the percentage of assets allocated to this sector may be as low as 10 percent. As an investor grows more in tune with foreign investing, the percentage may rise to 20 percent or more as market conditions dictate.

Some countries, such as Japan, have secondary stock markets. How important are these to the international investor?

That depends on the country. In Canada, the regional exchanges are quite different from one another and the savvy investor must understand the nuances. In Europe, old, long-established exchanges within the same country may have unique personalities. In Japan, the various exchanges follow the same rules and are similar. Many Japanese stocks trade on several exchanges simultaneously. Very knowledgeable investors who are able to assume a high level of risk sometimes find smaller growth stocks on secondary exchanges, but, ordinarily, the stocks found there are best left to mutual fund managers or other investors with expert research capabilities.

What are the traditional ways to measure the value of a stock?

Dividend yield, price to earnings ratio, and book value are the primary measures of value. Each tells something important about the value of a stock, especially when put into historical context or compared to other companies within the same industry. It is also important that a company's cash flow will cover all current and future debts.

Why is it important to follow stock market indicators?

All markets move in cycles, based upon natural, political, and other influences. In international stocks, choosing the right country at the right time is often more important than choosing an individual stock. By following market indicators over a long period of time, especially when depicted on a chart, it is easier to see how a market has been performing and in which direction it may be moving.

How does around-the-clock trading affect the individual investor?

Twenty-four hour trading, which is a virtual reality for certain large international stocks, has enormous implications for large-scale traders. Liquidity is increased, the possibility for arbitrage profits arise, and so forth. Occasionally, around-the-clock trading will let the impact of a cataclysmic or shocking event be quickly felt. For the smaller investor who tends to buy mutual funds or to buy and hold shares for the long-term, there sometimes is little impact on a day-to-day basis.

What is the difference between a global mutual fund and an international mutual fund?

A global equity fund invests in securities traded worldwide, including the United States. An international fund invests in securities of companies located outside the United States.

Is there a quick way to measure the risk of investing in a particular country?

To gauge risk, check certificate of deposit (CD) interest rates of the country in question. CD rates that are exceedingly high when compared to those of other countries indicate a high level of danger. Banks are forced to pay high rates to compensate for risk and to attract deposits.

Should I hedge my foreign investment portfolio in the currency market?

A. Only major traders need to consider hedging. Hedging itself carries an element of risk, and it is costly. Commissions must be paid for buying and selling currencies and on interest paid on any loans taken to cover the hedge.

What is the difference between gambling and speculation?

Gambling is based on random results, or the roll of the dice. Speculation is based on a calculated possibility of success, albeit linked to high risk. The speculator expects to receive outstanding profits in correlation with the level of risk. Anyone who invests in stocks on rumor, a casual recommendation, or without sufficient research and evaluation is gambling.

Must I pay taxes on investment earnings from foreign countries?

If you are a U.S. citizen or a resident alien of the United States, you must report these earnings, translated into U.S. dollars, to the Internal Revenue Service. If you have already paid taxes on the earnings in another country, that tax should be reported and in most cases will reduce the amount of tax due to the IRS.

How can an investor best keep informed about investment risks, conditions, and opportunities in foreign countries?

Thanks to electronics, satellites, and other mass communications technology, there is an abundance of information. International news on television and radio has improved in recent years, and virtually all business newspapers and magazines address international topics. *The Wall Street Journal, Barron's, Investor's Daily,* and other investment newspapers carry stock market indicators and stock quotations for markets outside the United States.

GLOSSARY

Arbitrage a maneuver by which an investor buys a security, currency, or some other commodity in one market for the purpose of immediately selling it for a higher price in one or more other markets.

Bearer form a stock registered to the "bearer," or to any person who physically holds it. The name of the owner is not registered with the issuing corporation. Coupons are attached to the certificate, and dividends are payable upon presentation of the coupon.

Bolsa stock exchange in Spanish-speaking countries.

Book value the worth of a company's tangible assets, minus liabilities, divided by the number of shares outstanding.

Borse (Bourse) stock exchanges in Germany and other European countries.

Capital financial resources, including various forms of monetary funding such as debt and equity.

Capital markets venues where capital is traded, including private placement circumstances and organized securities exchanges.

Central bank a national bank that conducts the business of a country and protects its public interests. The bank may issue currency, carry out monetary policy, hold reserve deposits of other banks, and so on. In the United States, these tasks are conducted by the Federal Reserve Bank.

Certificate of Deposit (CD) a time deposit that carries a guaranteed rate of return. In a federally insured bank in the United States, a CD is covered by deposit insurance.

Closed-end fund mutual funds with a set number of shares. When these shares are sold, closed-end funds trade on stock exchanges like corporate shares.

Currency exchange rate the price at which a nation's currency can be converted into another's. Exchange rates vary country to country, with many legal and market factors influencing the difference.

Currency forward a contract by which an investor agrees to accept delivery on a specific amount of foreign currency at the current price, to be delivered at a specific future date. These are traded on formal exchanges.

Currency futures similar to currency forward contracts.

Currency impact the effect that the fluctuation of one currency against another has on an investment. The rise of the dollar versus the yen, for example, will devalue any dollar investment previously made in Japan.

Currency option an option works much like a currency forward or a currency futures contract, except that the investor only pays for the right to buy the currency. He or she is not required to buy the currency at the time the contract is due. If the investor does not buy the money, the price paid for the option is forfeited. The option price is less than the full price of the currency.

Debt equity swap a technique used in Latin America and other regions to trade corporate debt for equity in the same company. The purpose is to relieve the companies and their banks of excessive debt burden.

Denationalization see privatization.

Diversification the spreading of funds among a number of different types of investments or securities to reduce the risks inherent in investing.

Dividend earnings paid per share of stock. In the United States, dividends are typically declared annually and paid quarterly. Practices may differ in other countries.

Dividend yield computed by dividing the dividend by the price of the share. Even if the share price does not rise as the investor hopes it will, he most likely will receive this minimum rate of return. Dividend yield is used as a measure of value of a stock.

Dollar denominated account bank, brokerage, or other accounts that are transacted in U.S. dollars.

Equity any investment that involves ownership.

European community (EC) the collective designation of three organizations with common membership: the European Economic Community (Common Market), the European Coal and Steel Community, and the European Atomic Energy Community (Euratom). The 12 full members are Belgium, Denmark, France, Germany, Greece, Ireland, Italy, Luxembourg, the Netherlands, Portugal, Spain, and the United Kingdom. Additional European nations have applied for membership and some 60 other countries are affiliated with the EC.

Fiscal policy federal taxation and spending policy, which is frequently adjusted to maintain a high employment level and economic growth.

Foreign currency account a bank, stock, or some other account denominated in the currency of another country. Foreign currency accounts are not allowed in all countries, and only became legal in the United States in 1989.

Forward Contract see futures contract.

Futures Contract the purchase or sale of an item—stock, bond, currency, commodity—at a price set at the time of the contract, but with delivery and settlement to take place at some future date. Futures contracts are bought and sold on formal exchanges.

Group of Seven (G-7) nations the world's major industrial democracies, whose leaders meet at intervals to discuss and sometimes react to global economic matters. The seven nations are Canada, France, Germany, Great Britain, Italy, Japan, and the United States.

Hard assets tangible resources such as real estate, automobiles, or gold.

Hedging placing an investment to offset the possibility of loss in another investment. For example: buying a foreign currency to compensate for possible exchange rate shifts when buying stocks in the same currency. Hedging is expensive. Interest must be paid on any borrowed dollars and commissions paid on currency sales.

Hyperinflation an inflation rate of 100 percent per year or more. Hyperinflation leads to economic chaos and, at times, collapse.

Inflation a rise in the price of goods and services.

Intangible assets financial assets such as stocks, bonds, or currencies. These also are called paper assets.

Liquidity the ease with which an asset is converted to cash. Because stocks and bonds can be sold readily in an open market, they are highly liquid. Real estate, which depends on proper market conditions and finding a willing buyer, is less liquid.

Managed economy any economy where political and economic policy, rather than market forces, dominate. All modern economies are managed to some extent.

Monetary policy Federal Reserve decisions to increase or decrease the money supply, or the amount of currency in circulation. Through various actions taken by the central bank, credit then becomes more readily available (thus stimulating the economy) or more difficult to obtain (curbing economic activity).

Mutual fund an investment company that pools money from shareholders and invests it. A mutual fund stands ready to buy back its shares at their current net asset value.

Nationalization the seizing of private assets, such as companies, for conversion to government ownership. This may occur with or without compensation to private owners.

Net Asset Value (NAV) the worth of a mutual fund's assets (securities, cash, and accrued earnings), minus its liabilities, divided by the number of shares outstanding.

Open-end funds a mutual fund that consists of a pool of funds with an unlimited number of shareholders. The fund's value fluctuates with the value of investments that have been made. These funds are listed together in the stock pages under mutual funds.

Option the right to buy or sell an asset for an agreed upon sum. If the option is not exercised by a predetermined date, the right expires and the option holder forfeits the payment.

Ordinary shares common stock in Great Britain.

Pink sheets a daily listing by the *National Quotation Bureau* of the bid and ask price of thousands of *over the* *counter* stocks that are not listed on the OTC markets or quoted in the newspaper. Generally these are very small companies.

Price/Earnings Ratio the price of a share divided by the earnings per share. Often used as a measure of value of a stock.

Privatization the conversion of government-owned assets, such as a company, to the hands of private investors. Also called denationalization.

Prospectus a document offered to the potential purchaser of a mutual fund or of a new security. Its purpose is to fully inform the investor as to the nature of the investment, the level of risk, and other important facts.

Protectionism a government practice of passing laws, setting tariffs, or engaging in other activities that give domestic products and services a marketplace advantage over those from other countries.

Recession an economic downturn, defined by most economists as two consecutive quarters of negative growth in the *Gross National Product.*

Selling short the sale of a stock or a commodity futures contract that the seller does not yet own. A short sale is a technique used for various purposes, most commonly to take advantage of an anticipated drop in price. The seller delivers a borrowed security, which he must buy later. If the price has declined when the purchase date arrives, the seller makes a profit. If the price has increased, the investor loses money.

Settlement the actual payment for a stock or some other financial product that has been traded on an exchange.

Spread a difference in price or yield of the same or similar asset. The difference between the price of the same currency in two different markets would be called the spread; the difference in yield between a long-term government security and a high quality corporate security of a similar maturity is called the spread.

Street name stock held in the name of the brokerage house, rather than that of the actual owner. By holding the shares in street name, investors can sell the stock quickly and more easily, because the stock certificate need not be signed, certified, and delivered to the brokerage.

Total return for a common stock, this equals share price growth plus dividends paid.

Yield curve the relationship between yield and maturity for an interest-bearing security. Ordinarily the yield increases as the term lengthens, to compensate investors for incremental risk. On a chart depicting such a market, the plotted line is near the bottom for short-term securities and rises as maturity lengthens. In uncertain markets, the curve skews. Investors generally seek the highest yield possible for the shortest maturity possible. A yield curve demonstrates what maturity and interest rate offers the greatest advantage.

INDEX

135